CUT AND CREATE!

Spring & Summer

EASY STEP-BY-STEP PROJECTS THAT TEACH SCISSOR SKILLS

Written by Mary Tucker

Illustrated by Kim Rankin

Teaching & Learning Company

1204 Buchanan St., P.O. Box 10

Carthage, IL 62321-0010

This book belongs to

_____

Printing No. 987654321

Teaching & Learning Company
1204 Buchanan St., P.O. Box 10
Carthage, IL 62321-0010

TABLE OF CONTENTS

Easy Projects

Moderate Projects

Challenging Projects

TLC10535 Copyright © Teaching & Learning Company, Carthage, IL 62321-0010

Dear Teacher or Family,

"I did it myself" is a phrase that can be the foundation for a lifetime of accomplishment and positive self-esteem.

Cut and Create activities can be used to develop a variety of important early skills and to provide projects in which children can take pride and succeed.

- Simple patterns and easy, step-by-step directions develop scissor skills and give practice in visual-motor coordination. The scissor rating system in the upper right-hand corner on the first page of each project quickly identifies easy (✂), moderate (✂ ✂) and challenging (✂ ✂ ✂) projects.
- Materials used are inexpensive and readily available.
- Finished products are fun, colorful and can be used for everything from play items to props; room decorations for walls, bulletin boards or mobiles; learning center manipulatives for counting, sorting, classifying or labeling; gifts or favors for parties or guests; and much more.

The simple and fun activities included in this book will help young learners build a solid base for a variety of skills such as: following directions, observation, discrimination and information processing. A variety of learning styles is addressed including visual, auditory and tactile.

Your art program, whether structured or serendipitous, can benefit from these simple and sequenced scissor skill activities. Your students will

- develop manual dexterity
- communicate
- learn to control their environment by being responsible for tools and materials
- observe
- discriminate (by color, shape, texture)
- sort, order, group and engage in other math processes
- imagine!

We hope you and your students will enjoy these projects. They have been designed to stimulate learning and creativity in a way that is simple and fun. So go cut and create—and have a good time!

Sincerely,

Mary Kim

Mary Tucker and Kim Rankin

BEACH TOYS

Materials: *white, orange, light green, dark green, blue and yellow paper; scissors; glue; black crayon or marker*

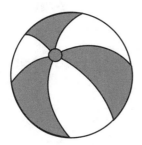

1 Cut one #1 ball from white paper. Cut one each of #2, #3 and #4 stripes and one #5 button from orange paper. Glue the stripes on the ball as shown. Glue the button on the top of the ball where the stripes meet.

2 Cut two #6 shoes from light green paper. Cut two #7 straps from dark green paper. Turn one shoe and one strap over so there is a right and left. Use a black crayon or marker to draw a sole on each shoe as shown. Glue the straps near the top of the shoes. Glue the shoes together as shown. Then glue the left shoe to the ball.

3 Cut one #8 pail and one #9 handle from blue paper. Glue the handle on the pail. Glue the ball and shoes to the bottom of the pail as shown.

4 Cut one #10 star from yellow paper. Glue the star on the pail as shown.

Beach Toys

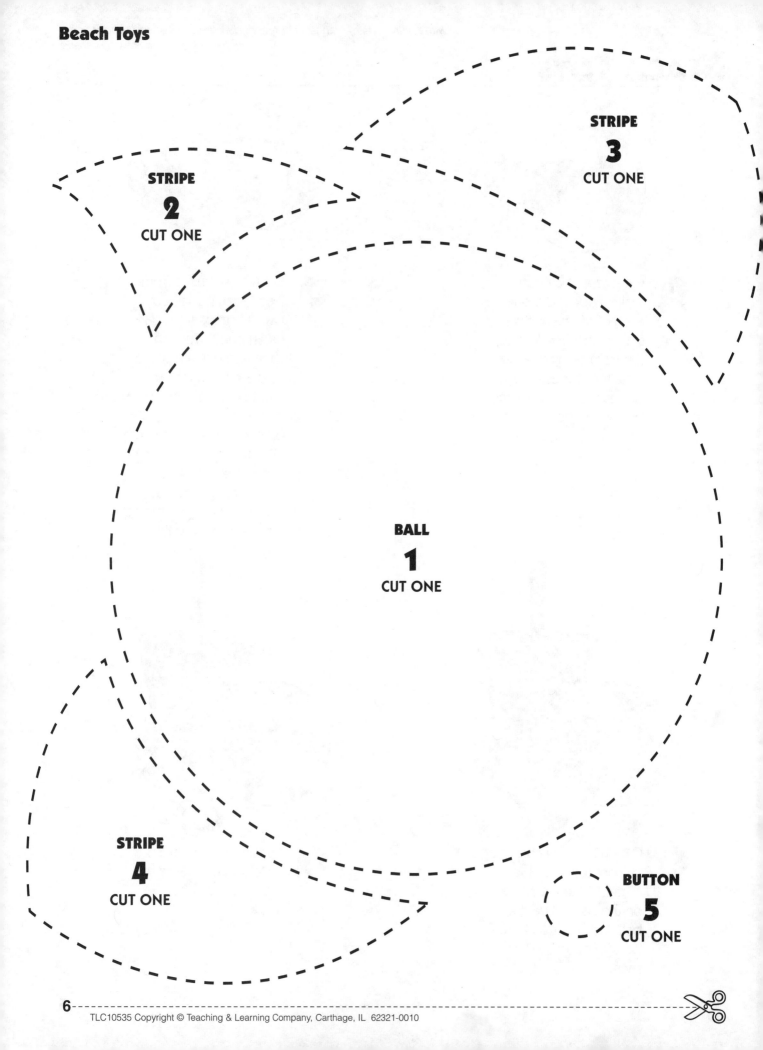

STRIPE
2
CUT ONE

STRIPE
3
CUT ONE

BALL
1
CUT ONE

STRIPE
4
CUT ONE

BUTTON
5
CUT ONE

Beach Toys

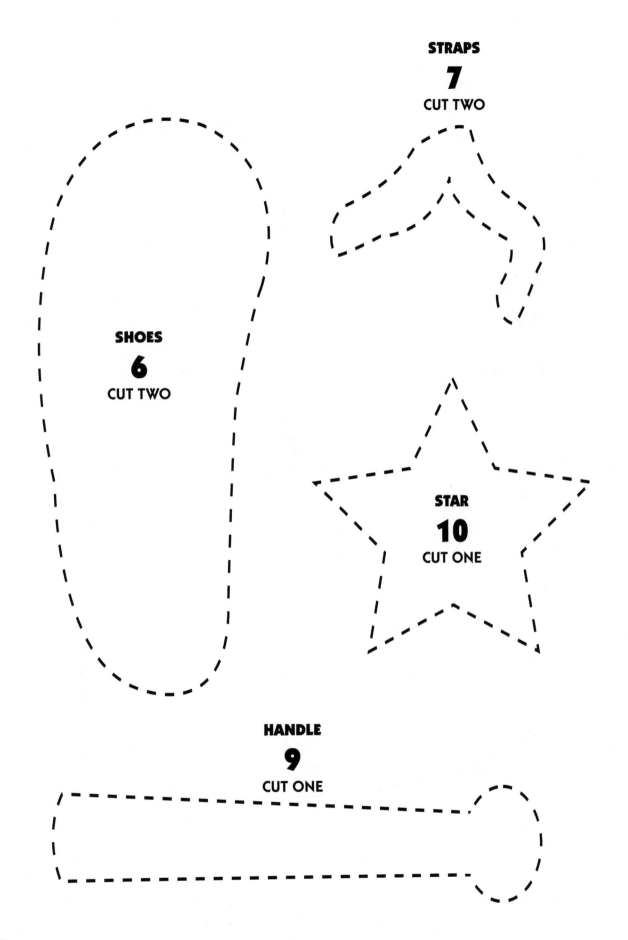

STRAPS
7
CUT TWO

SHOES
6
CUT TWO

STAR
10
CUT ONE

HANDLE
9
CUT ONE

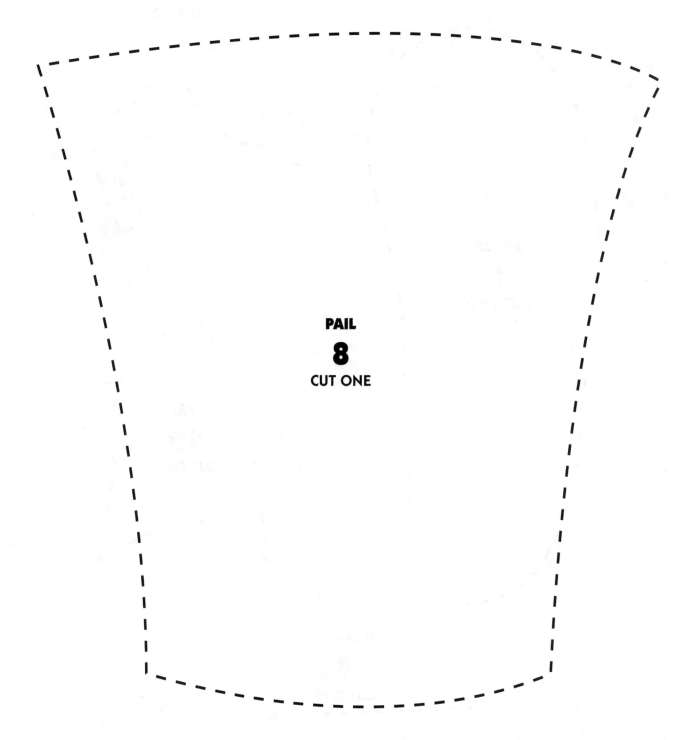

PAIL

8

CUT ONE

CINCO DE MAYO HAT

Materials: *yellow, red and green paper; scissors; glue; black crayon or marker*

1 Cut one #1 front and one #2 back from yellow paper. Glue the two pieces together as shown. Use a black crayon or marker to print *CINCO DE MAYO* on the front of the hat.

2 Cut one #3 top from yellow paper. Glue it at the center of the hat as shown.

3 Cut five #4 triangles from red paper. Glue them around the top of the hat as shown.

4 Cut several #5 circles from green paper. Glue the circles on both sides of the hat brim as shown.

Cinco de Mayo Hat

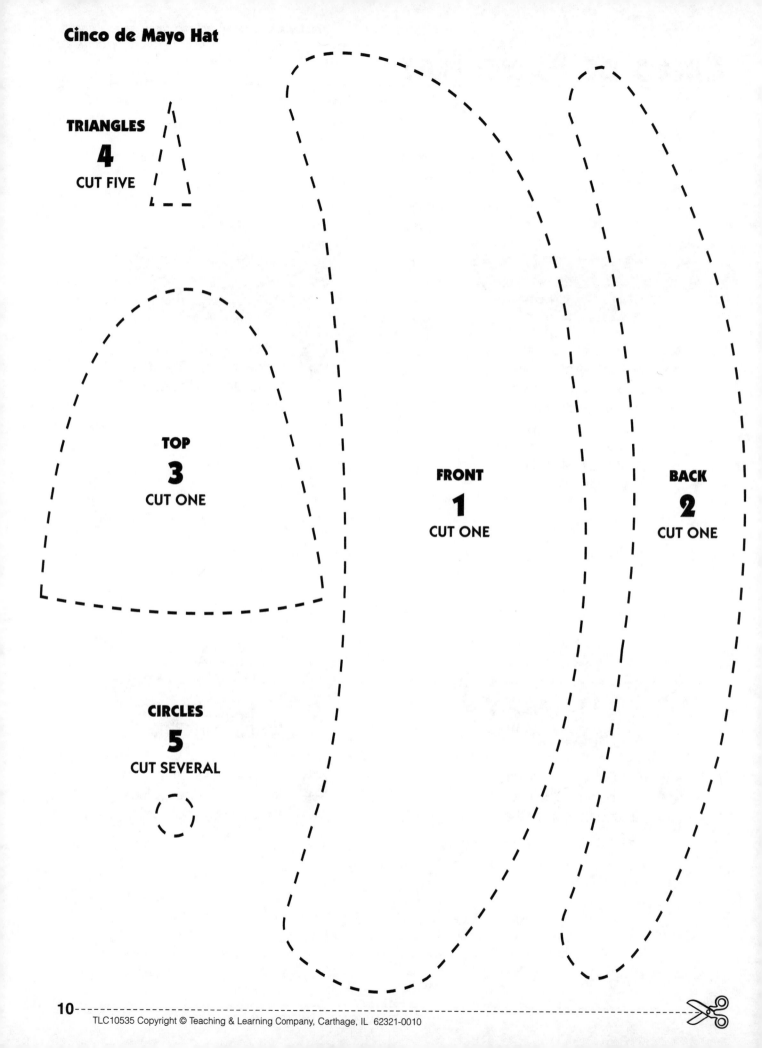

TRIANGLES
4
CUT FIVE

TOP
3
CUT ONE

FRONT
1
CUT ONE

BACK
2
CUT ONE

CIRCLES
5
CUT SEVERAL

ICE CREAM CONE

Materials: orange, brown, pink and red paper; scissors; glue; black crayon or marker

1 Cut one #1 cone from orange paper. Use a black crayon or marker to draw lines on the cone as shown.

2 Cut one #2 ice cream from brown paper. Glue the ice cream on the top of the cone.

3 Cut one #2 ice cream from pink paper. Glue the pink ice cream on the top of the brown ice cream.

4 Cut one #3 cherry from red paper. Glue the cherry on the top of the pink ice cream.

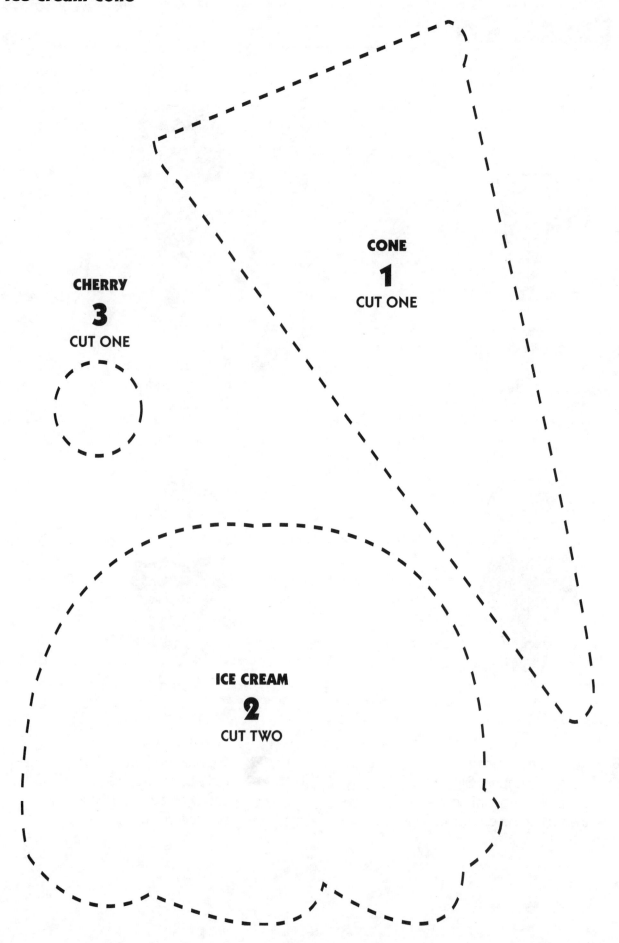

CONE

1

CUT ONE

CHERRY

3

CUT ONE

ICE CREAM

2

CUT TWO

KITE

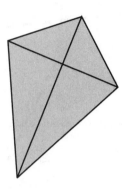

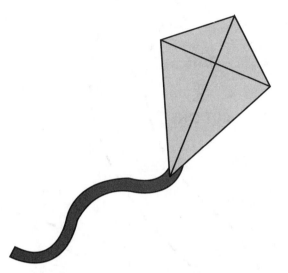

1 Cut one #1 kite from yellow paper. Use a black crayon or marker to draw lines on the kite as shown.

2 Cut one #2 tail from blue paper. Glue the tail to the back of the kite at the bottom.

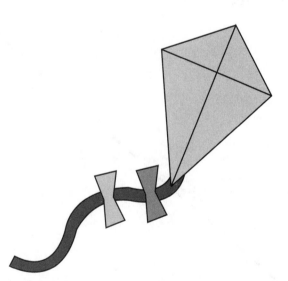

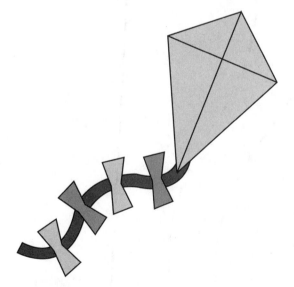

3 Cut four #3 bows, two from orange paper and two more from green paper. Glue two of the bows to the kite tail.

4 Glue the other two bows to the kite tail as shown.

Kite

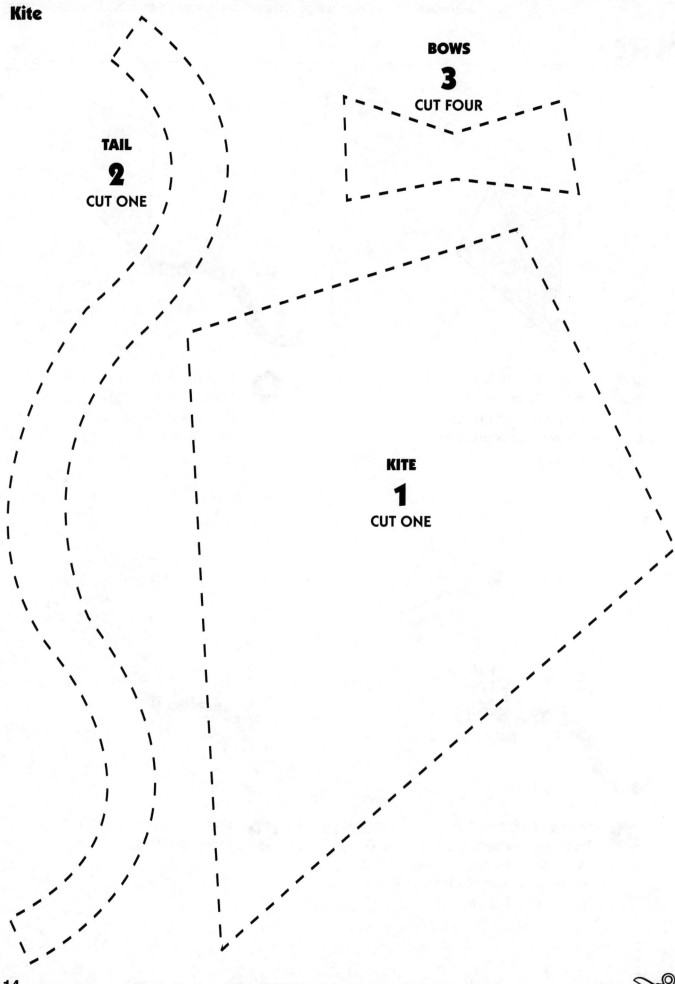

BOWS

3

CUT FOUR

TAIL

2

CUT ONE

KITE

1

CUT ONE

Kite

Materials: *red, brown, yellow and light blue paper; scissors; glue; black crayon or marker*

RAINY DAY UMBRELLA

1 Cut one #1 umbrella from red paper. Use a black crayon or marker to draw lines on the umbrella as shown.

2 Cut one #2 pole from brown paper. Glue the pole to the back of the umbrella, at the bottom, as shown.

3 Cut one #3 handle and one #4 top from yellow paper. Glue the handle to the bottom of the umbrella pole and the top to the center top, as shown.

4 Cut several #5 raindrops from light blue paper. Glue the raindrops onto the umbrella.

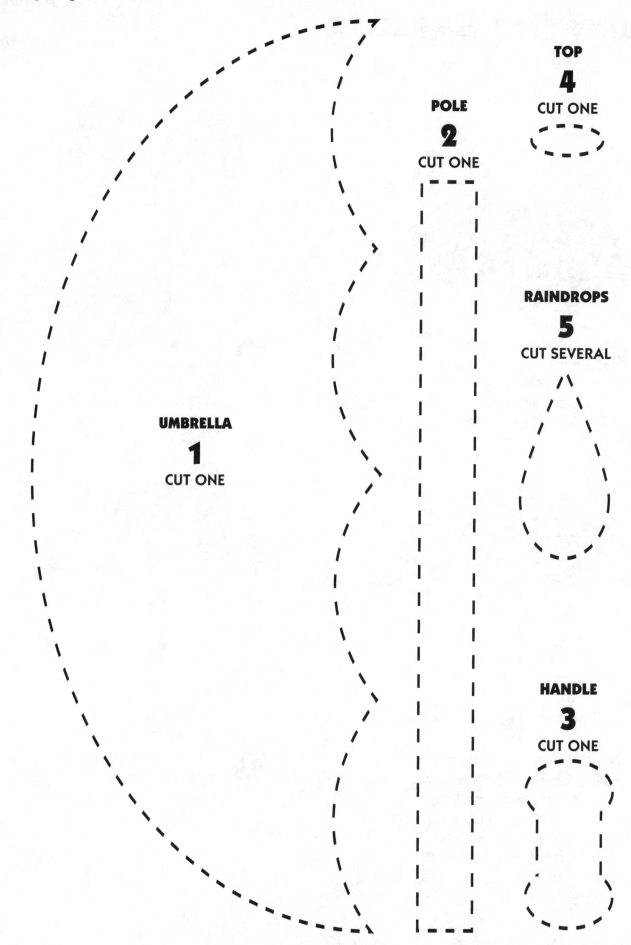

TOP

4

CUT ONE

POLE

2

CUT ONE

RAINDROPS

5

CUT SEVERAL

UMBRELLA

1

CUT ONE

HANDLE

3

CUT ONE

SPRING TULIP

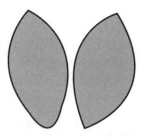

1 Cut two #1 tulip sides from red paper.

2 Cut one #2 tulip center from red paper. Glue the center and the two sides together as shown. Use a black crayon or marker to draw lines on the flower as shown.

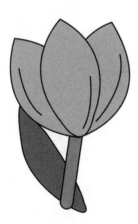

3 Cut one #3 stem from green paper. Glue the stem to the bottom of the tulip as shown. Cut one #4 leaf from green paper. Glue it behind the stem near the bottom as shown.

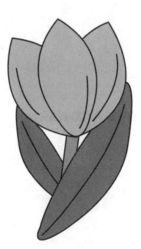

4 Cut one #5 leaf from green paper. Glue the leaf to the front of the stem. Use a black crayon or marker to draw lines on the leaves as shown.

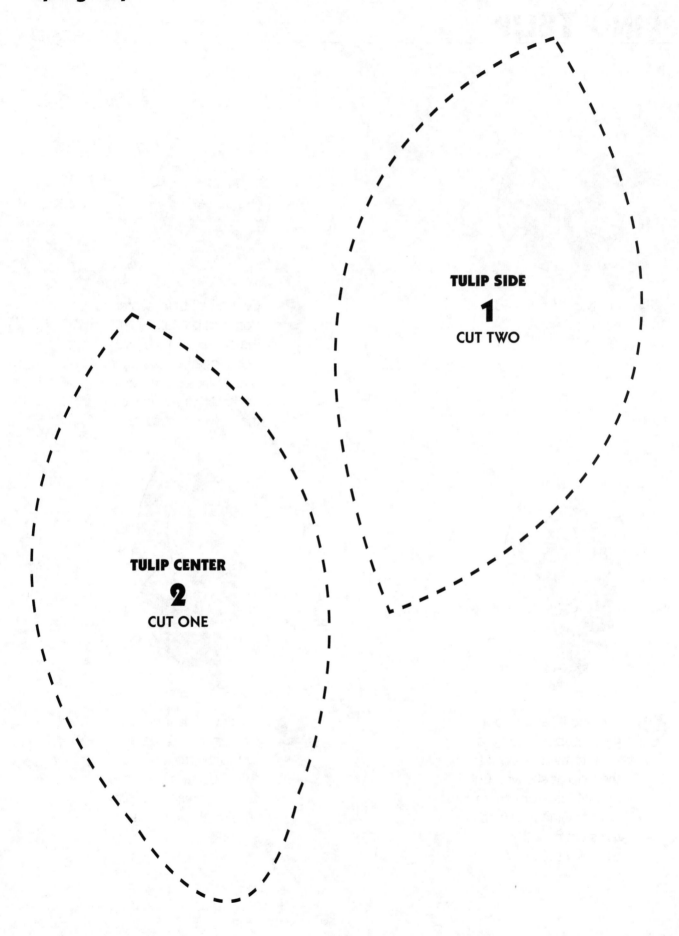

TULIP SIDE

1

CUT TWO

TULIP CENTER

2

CUT ONE

Spring Tulip

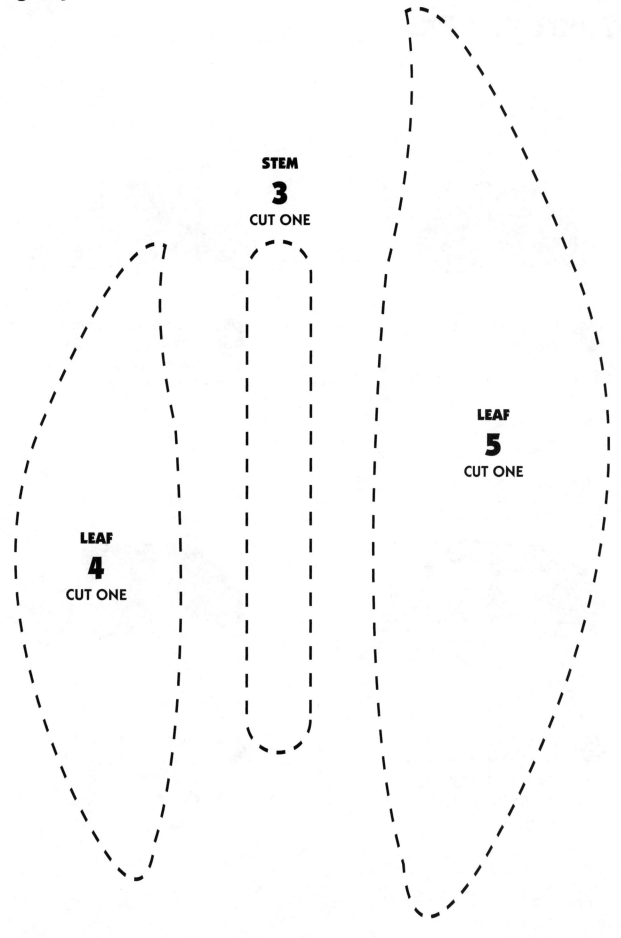

STEM

3

CUT ONE

LEAF

5

CUT ONE

LEAF

4

CUT ONE

STORM CLOUDS

1 Cut one #1 cloud from dark gray paper.

2 Cut one #2 cloud from light gray paper. Glue the two clouds together as shown.

3 Cut one #3 lightning bolt from yellow paper. Glue the top of the lightning bolt to the #1 cloud as shown.

4 Cut several #4 raindrops from light blue paper. Glue them on the clouds.

Storm Clouds

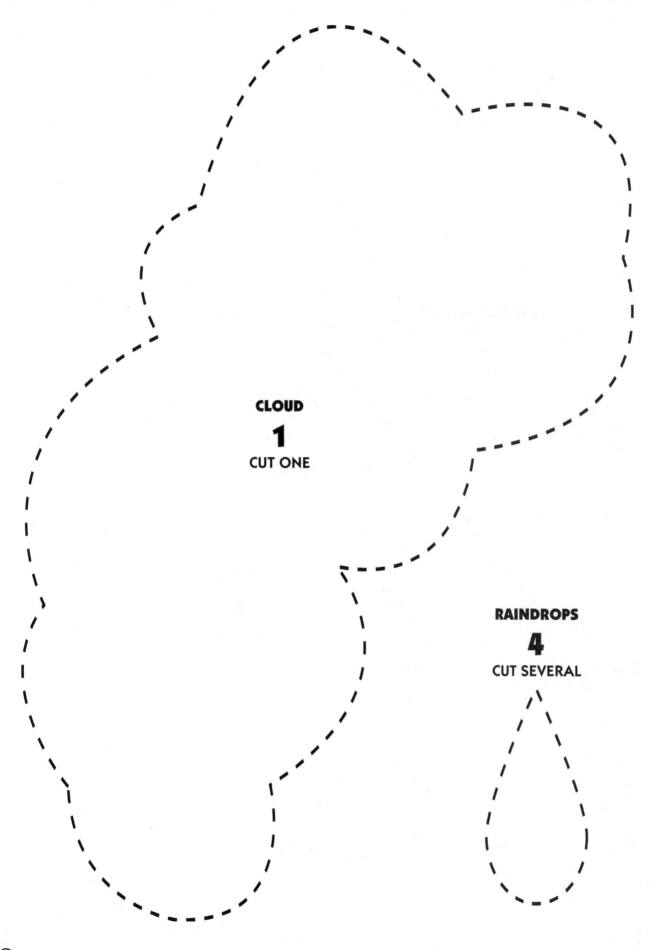

CLOUD

1

CUT ONE

RAINDROPS

4

CUT SEVERAL

Storm Clouds

LIGHTNING BOLT

3

CUT ONE

CLOUD

2

CUT ONE

Materials: *red, green and black paper; scissors; glue*

STRAWBERRY

1 Cut one #1 strawberry from red paper.

2 Cut one #2 leaf from green paper. Glue the leaf on the top of the strawberry.

3 Cut one #3 stem from green paper. Glue the stem on the leaf as shown.

4 Cut several #4 seeds from black paper. Glue the seeds on the strawberry.

Strawberry

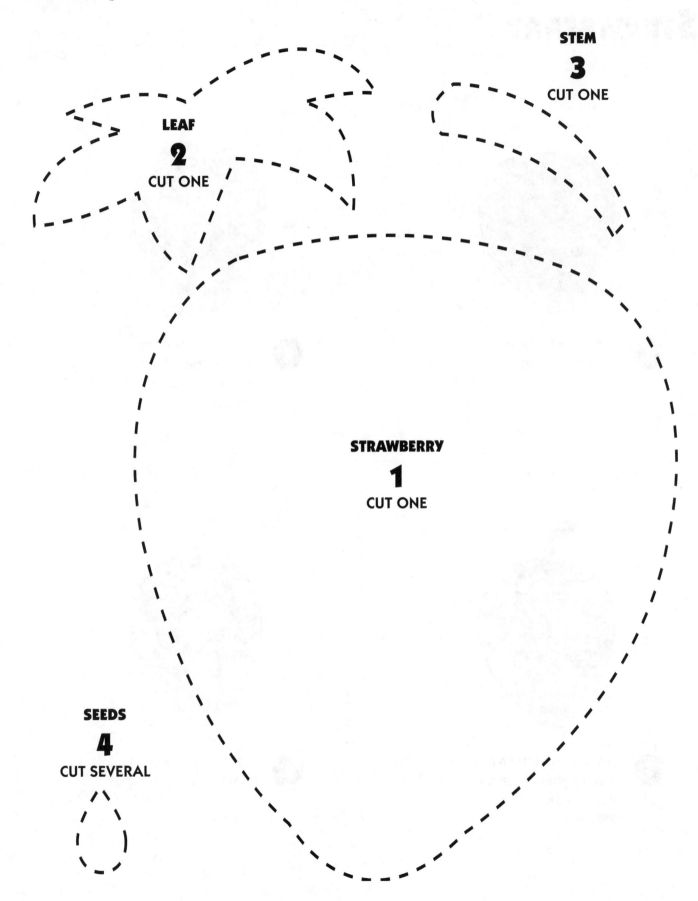

STEM

3

CUT ONE

LEAF

2

CUT ONE

STRAWBERRY

1

CUT ONE

SEEDS

4

CUT SEVERAL

SUN

1 Cut one #1 sun from orange paper.

2 Cut one #2 center from yellow paper. Glue the yellow center on the orange sun.

3 Cut two #3 eyes from white paper. Glue them on the sun. Cut two #4 pupils from black paper. Glue them on the #3 eyes as shown.

4 Cut one #5 nose from orange paper. Glue the nose under the eyes on the sun's face. Use a black crayon or marker to draw a smiling mouth on the sun.

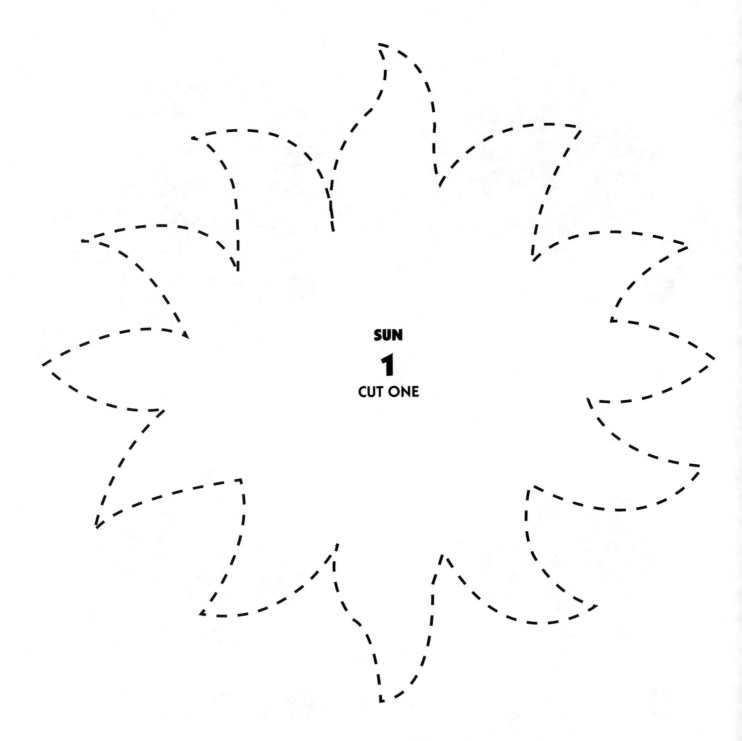

SUN

1

CUT ONE

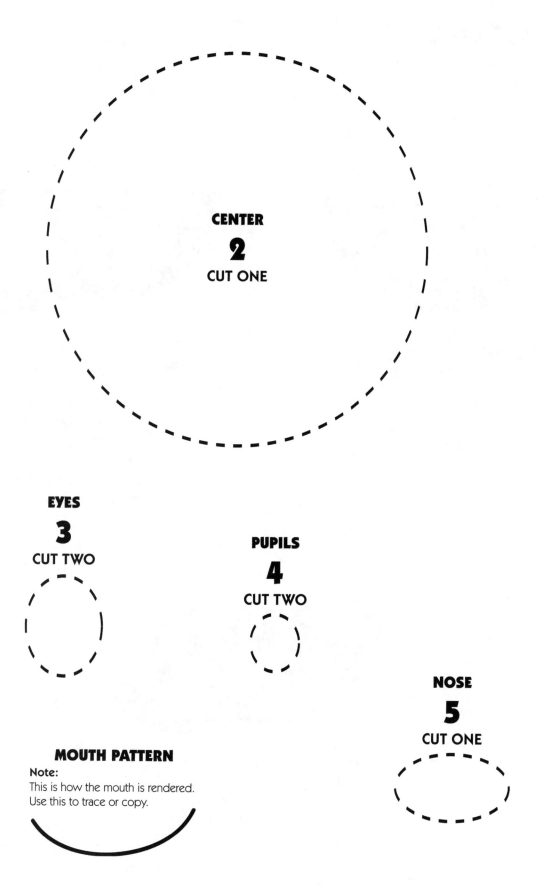

CENTER

2

CUT ONE

EYES

3

CUT TWO

PUPILS

4

CUT TWO

NOSE

5

CUT ONE

MOUTH PATTERN

Note:
This is how the mouth is rendered.
Use this to trace or copy.

Materials: *green, red and black paper; scissors; glue;*

WATERMELON

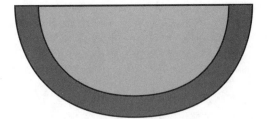

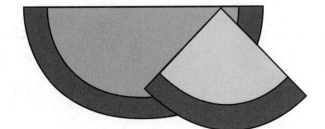

1 Cut one #1 half rind from green paper. Cut one #2 half melon from red paper. Glue the red melon on the rind, leaving an even green edge all around.

2 Cut one #3 quarter rind from green paper. Cut one #4 quarter melon from red paper. Glue the melon on the rind as you did in step 1. Glue the quarter piece of melon on the right side of the half melon.

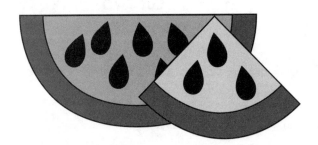

3 Cut several #5 seeds from black paper. Glue the seeds on the two pieces of watermelon as shown.

Watermelon

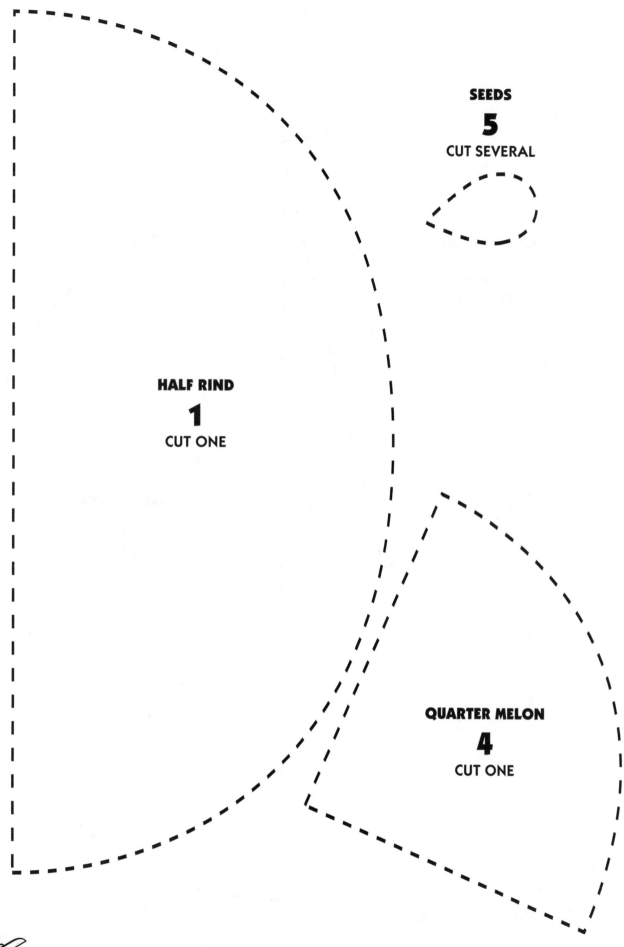

SEEDS

5

CUT SEVERAL

HALF RIND

1

CUT ONE

QUARTER MELON

4

CUT ONE

Watermelon

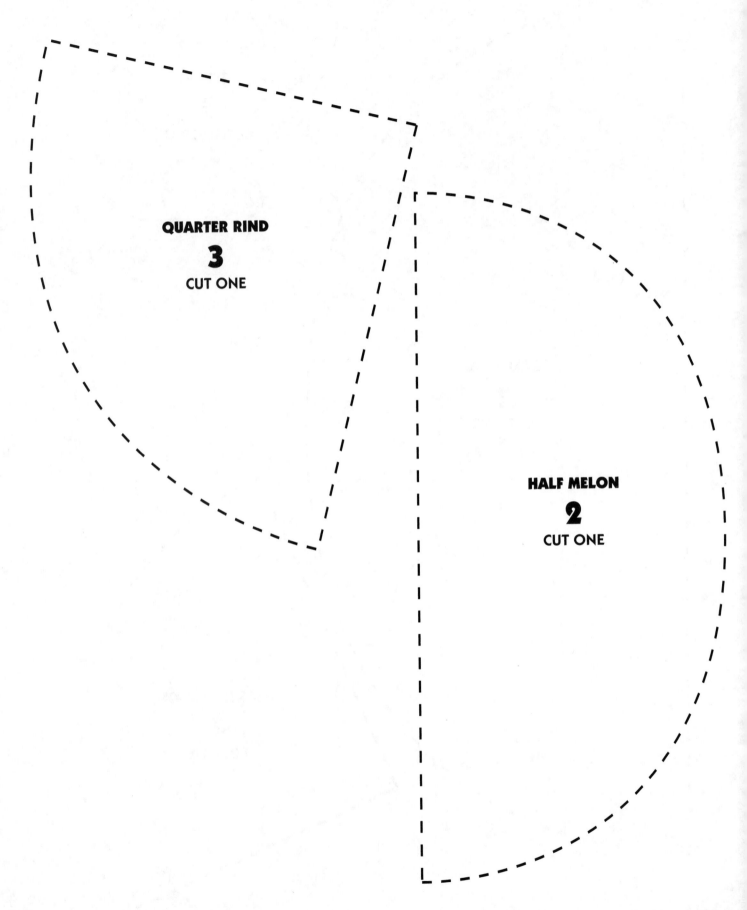

QUARTER RIND
3
CUT ONE

HALF MELON
2
CUT ONE

TLC10535 Copyright © Teaching & Learning Company, Carthage, IL 62321-0010

BABY RACCOON

Materials: brown or gray, white, black and pink paper; scissors; glue; black crayon or marker

1 Cut one #1 head from brown or gray paper. Cut one #2 lower face from white paper. Glue the lower face to the bottom of the head as shown.

2 Cut one #3 mask from black paper. Glue the mask above the lower face as shown.

3 Cut one #4 left ear and one #5 right ear from pink paper. Glue them in place as shown. Cut one #6 nose from black paper. Glue the nose on the face. Use a black crayon or marker to draw the mouth as shown.

4 Cut two #7 eyes from white paper and two #8 pupils from black paper. Glue the black pupils on the white eyes. Then glue them on the raccoon's mask as shown.

Baby Raccoon

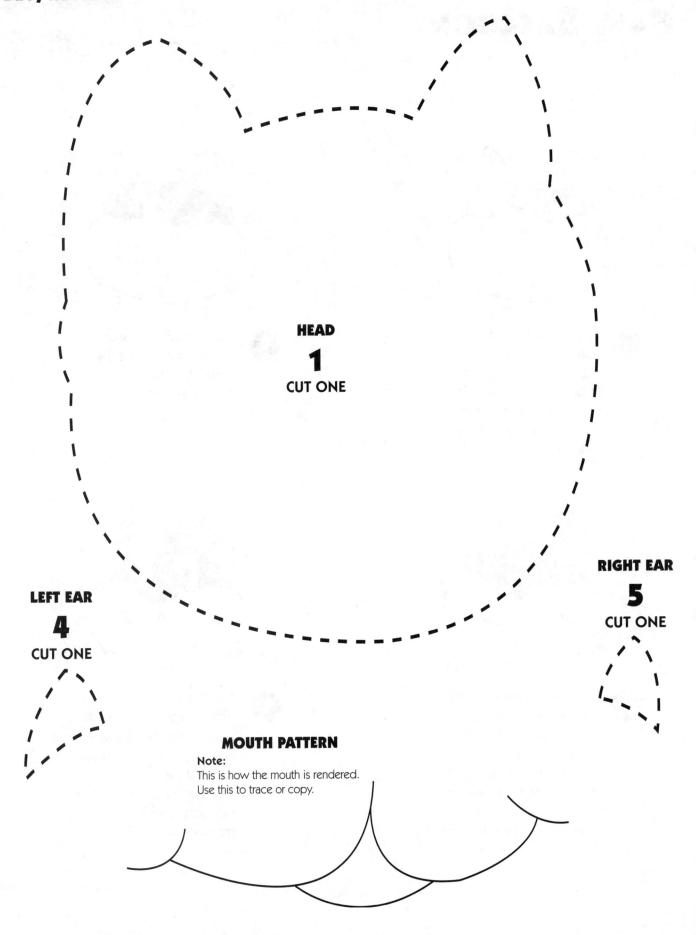

HEAD

1

CUT ONE

RIGHT EAR

5

CUT ONE

LEFT EAR

4

CUT ONE

MOUTH PATTERN

Note:
This is how the mouth is rendered.
Use this to trace or copy.

Baby Raccoon

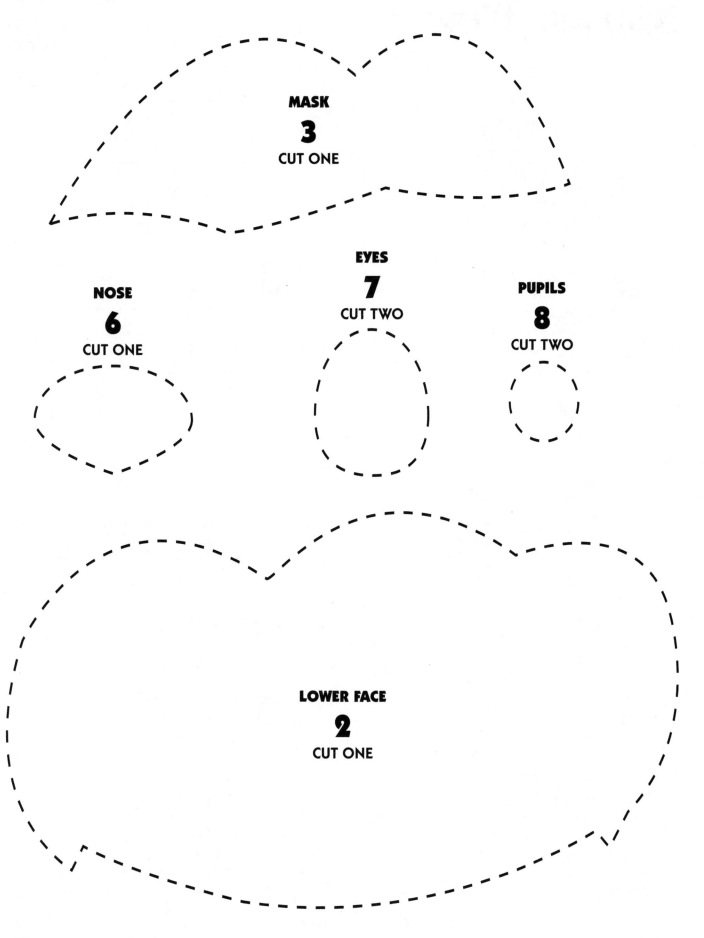

MASK
3
CUT ONE

EYES
7
CUT TWO

NOSE
6
CUT ONE

PUPILS
8
CUT TWO

LOWER FACE
2
CUT ONE

BIRD AND WORM

Materials: blue, orange, brown, white and black paper; scissors; glue; black crayon or marker

1 Cut one #1 body from blue paper. Cut one #2 beak from orange paper. Glue the beak to the body. Use a black crayon or marker to draw lines on the beak as shown.

2 Cut one #3 right wing and one #4 left wing from blue paper. Glue the right wing on the back of the body as shown. Glue the left wing on the front of the body as shown.

3 Cut two #5 feet from orange paper and one #6 tail from blue paper. Glue the two feet at the bottom of the body. Glue the tail at the end of the body. Use a black crayon or marker to draw lines on the feet as shown.

4 Cut one #7 worm from brown paper. Use a black crayon or marker to draw a face on the worm. Glue the worm in the bird's beak as shown. Cut one #8 eye from white paper. Glue it on the head. Cut one #9 pupil from black paper. Glue it on the #8 eye as shown.

Bird and Worm

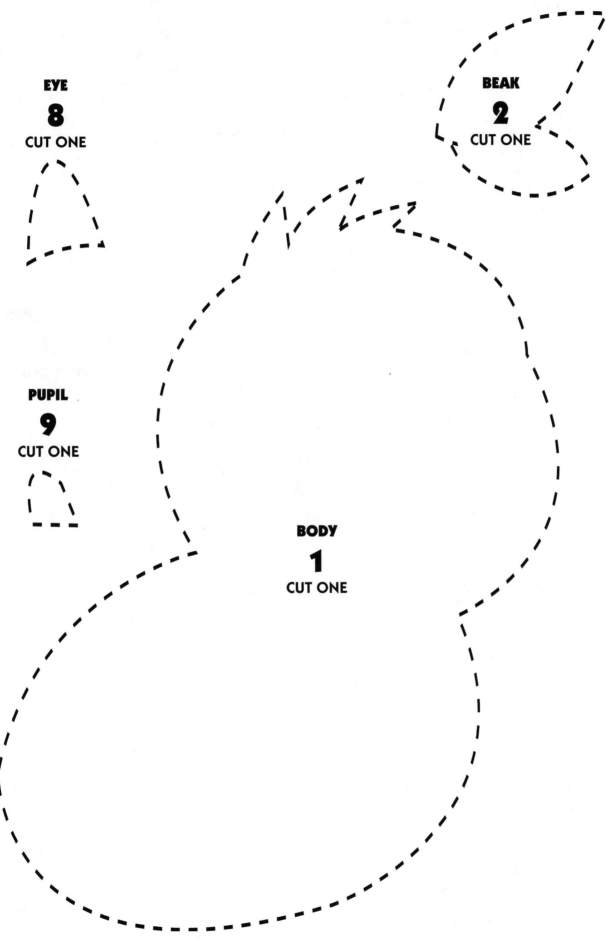

EYE
8
CUT ONE

BEAK
2
CUT ONE

PUPIL
9
CUT ONE

BODY
1
CUT ONE

Bird and Worm

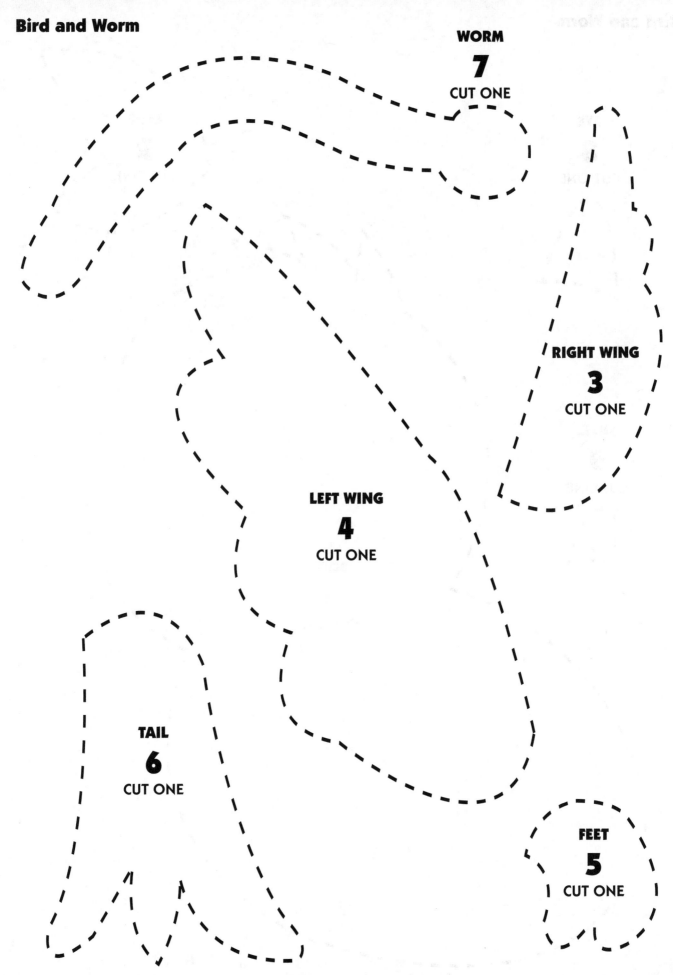

WORM
7
CUT ONE

RIGHT WING
3
CUT ONE

LEFT WING
4
CUT ONE

TAIL
6
CUT ONE

FEET
5
CUT ONE

BLOSSOMING TREE

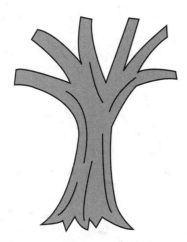

1 Cut one #1 tree trunk from brown paper. Use a black crayon or marker to draw lines on the tree trunk as shown.

2 Cut several #2 leaves from green paper. Glue the leaves on the limbs of the tree as shown. Use a black crayon or marker to draw lines on the leaves.

3 Cut several #3 blossoms from pink paper. Glue the blossoms on the tree. Use a black crayon or marker to draw a center on each blossom as shown.

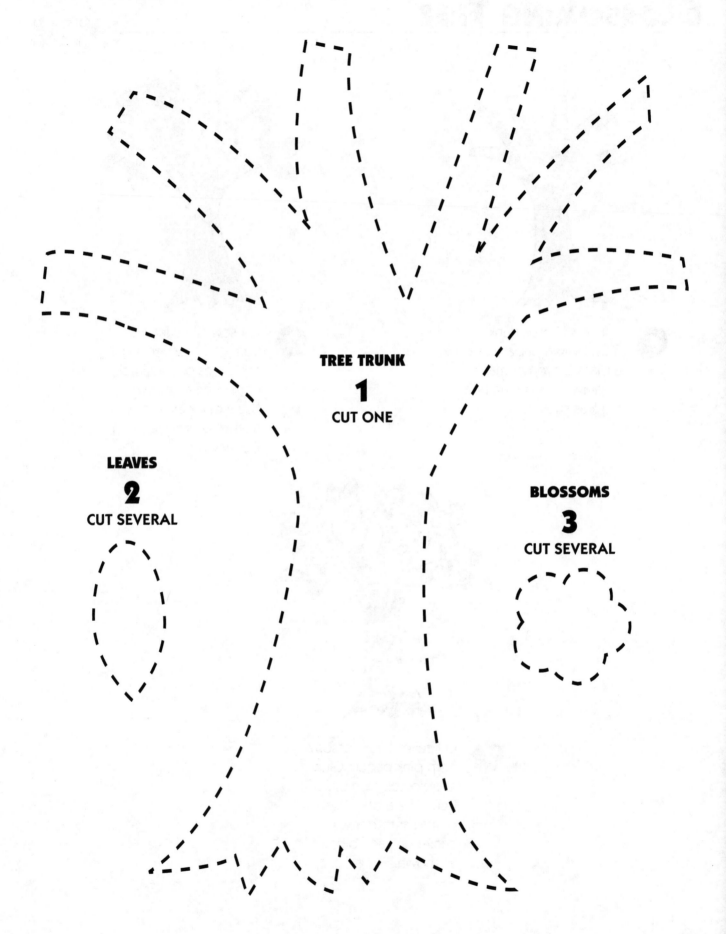

TREE TRUNK

1

CUT ONE

LEAVES

2

CUT SEVERAL

BLOSSOMS

3

CUT SEVERAL

DUCK IN A PUDDLE

Materials: *yellow, orange, blue, white and black paper; scissors; glue; black crayon or marker*

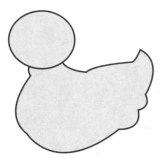

1 Cut one each of #1 body and #2 head from yellow paper. Glue the head on the body as shown.

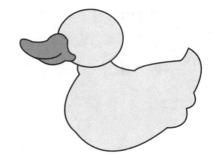

2 Cut one #3 beak from orange paper. Glue the beak on the left side of the head. Use a black crayon or marker to draw a smile on the beak as shown.

3 Cut two #4 feet from orange paper and one #5 wing from yellow paper. Glue the feet to the bottom of the body and glue the wing to the center of the body, as shown.

4 Cut one #6 puddle from blue paper. Glue the duck on the puddle as shown. Cut one #7 eye from white paper. Glue it on the duck's head. Cut one #8 pupil from black paper. Glue it on the #7 eye as shown.

Duck in a Puddle

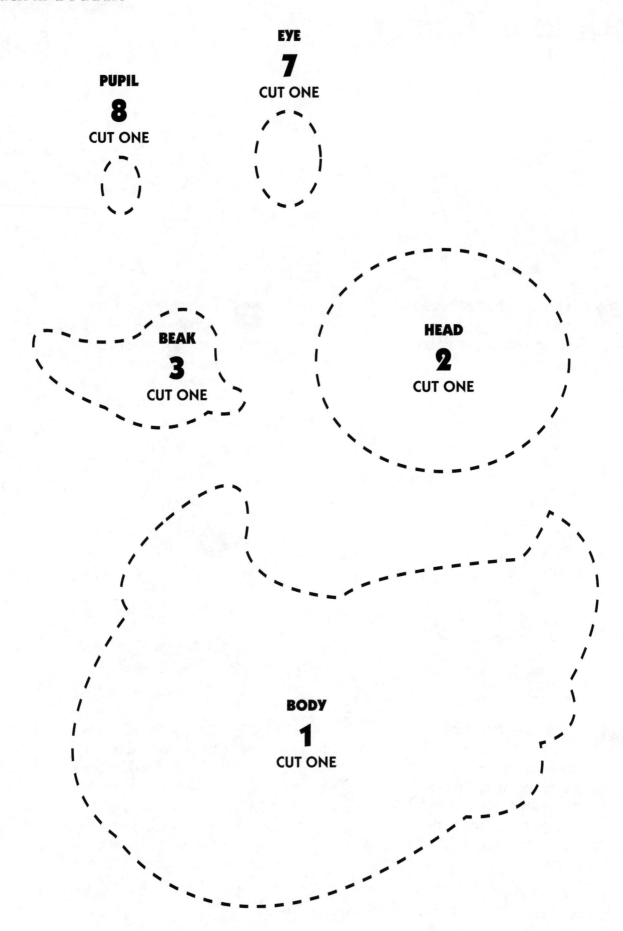

PUPIL
8
CUT ONE

EYE
7
CUT ONE

BEAK
3
CUT ONE

HEAD
2
CUT ONE

BODY
1
CUT ONE

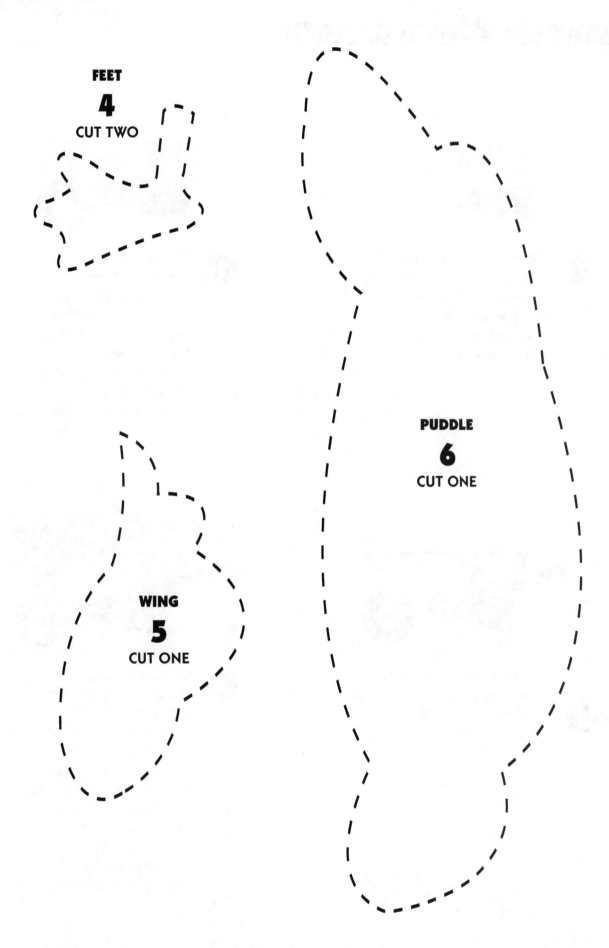

FEET
4
CUT TWO

PUDDLE
6
CUT ONE

WING
5
CUT ONE

GARDEN WHEELBARROW

Materials: red, black, white, brown, green and yellow paper; scissors; glue; black crayon or marker

1 Cut one #1 wheelbarrow from red paper and one #2 leg from black paper. Glue the leg to the bottom of the wheelbarrow as shown.

2 Cut one #3 wheel from black paper and one #4 center wheel from white paper. Glue the center wheel to the middle of the black wheel. Then glue the complete wheel to the front of the wheelbarrow, as shown.

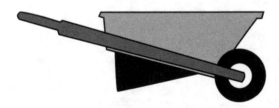

3 Cut one #5 handle from brown paper. Glue the handle on the wheelbarrow as shown.

4 Cut several #6 corn shucks from green paper. Cut several #7 ears of corn from yellow paper, one for each shuck. Use a black crayon or marker to draw lines on the corn as shown. Glue each ear of corn on a green shuck. Glue the corn sticking out of the wheelbarrow as shown.

Garden Wheelbarrow

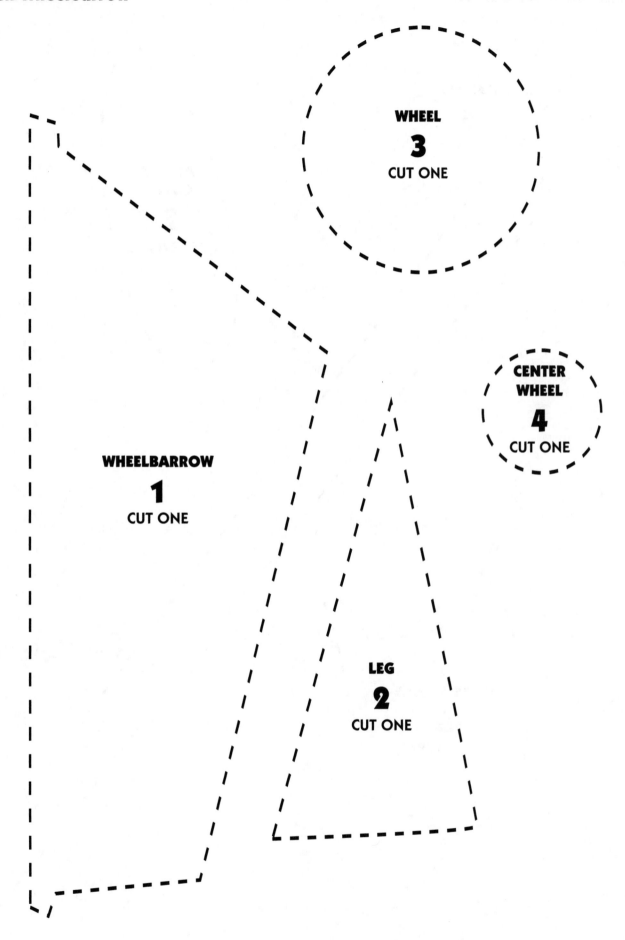

WHEEL
3
CUT ONE

CENTER
WHEEL
4
CUT ONE

WHEELBARROW
1
CUT ONE

LEG
2
CUT ONE

Garden Wheelbarrow

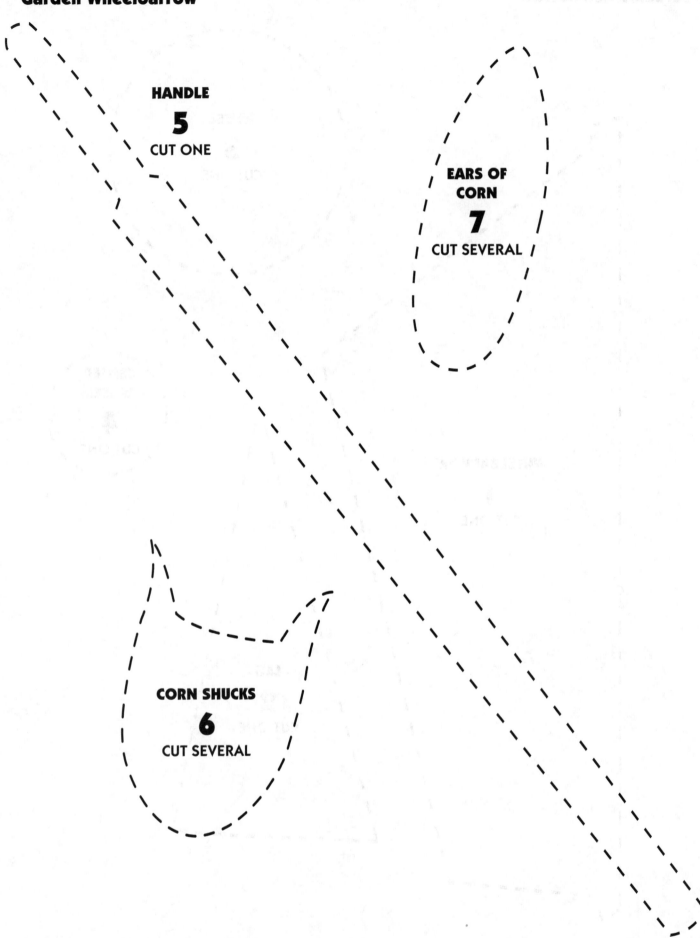

HANDLE

5

CUT ONE

EARS OF CORN

7

CUT SEVERAL

CORN SHUCKS

6

CUT SEVERAL

PATRIOTIC HAT

Materials: *white, red, blue and yellow paper; scissors; glue; black crayon or marker*

1 Cut one each of #1 hat and #2 brim from white paper. Glue the brim on the bottom of the hat.

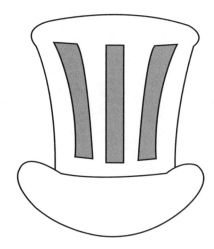

2 Cut one set of #3 stripes from red paper. Glue the stripes on the hat as shown.

3 Cut one #4 top from white paper. Glue it to the top of the hat.

4 Cut one #5 band from blue paper. Glue it on the hat brim as shown. Cut one #6 big star and two #7 small stars from yellow paper. Glue them on the hat band with the big star in the middle and a small star on each side of it.

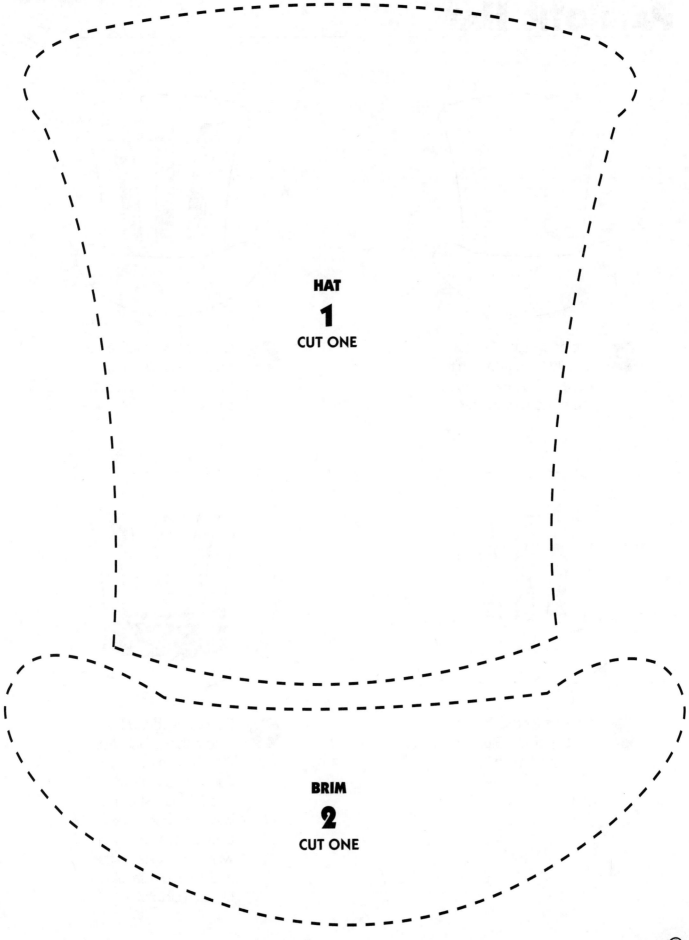

HAT

1

CUT ONE

BRIM

2

CUT ONE

Patriotic Hat

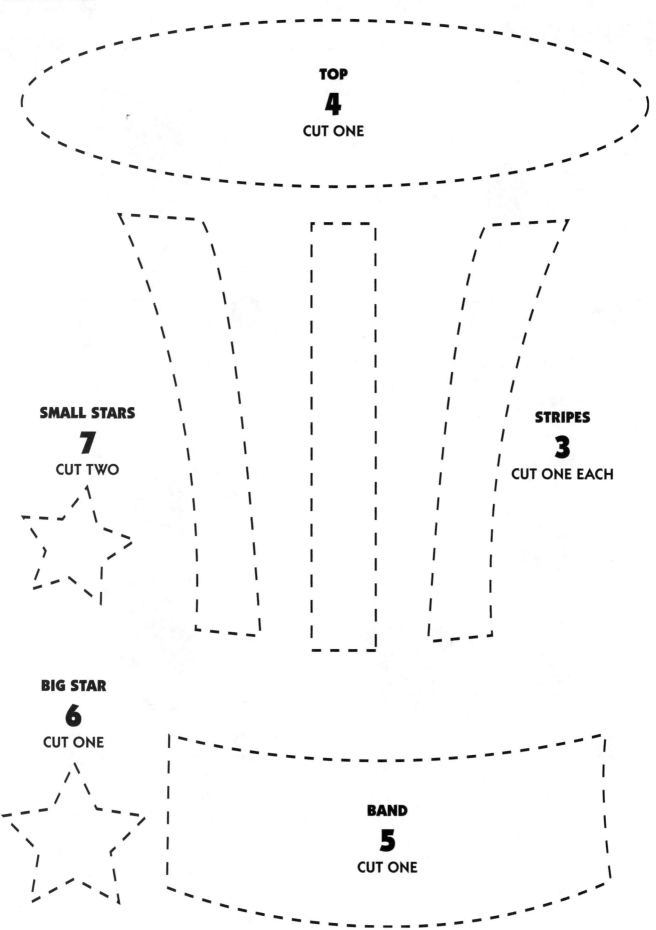

TOP
4
CUT ONE

SMALL STARS
7
CUT TWO

STRIPES
3
CUT ONE EACH

BIG STAR
6
CUT ONE

BAND
5
CUT ONE

Materials: brown, black, yellow, green and orange paper; scissors; glue; black crayon or marker

SUNFLOWER

1 Cut one #1 center from brown paper. Cut several #2 seeds from black paper. Glue them on the center. Cut seven #3 petals from yellow paper. Glue the petals around the center as shown.

2 Cut one #4 stem from green paper. Glue the stem to the flower as shown.

3 Cut one #5 pot from orange paper. Cut one #6 inside pot from brown paper. Glue the inside pot piece to the rim of the pot. Use a black crayon or marker to draw a line on the pot as shown.

4 Cut two #7 leaves from green paper. Glue a leaf on each side of the stem. Use a black crayon or marker to draw lines on the leaves. Glue the completed sunflower on the pot as shown.

Sunflower

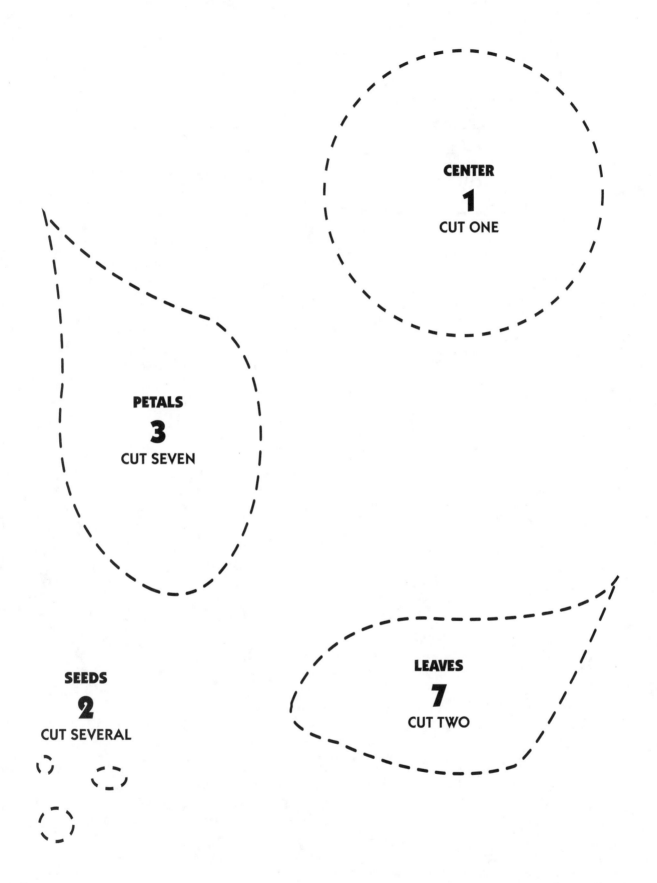

CENTER
1
CUT ONE

PETALS
3
CUT SEVEN

SEEDS
2
CUT SEVERAL

LEAVES
7
CUT TWO

Sunflower

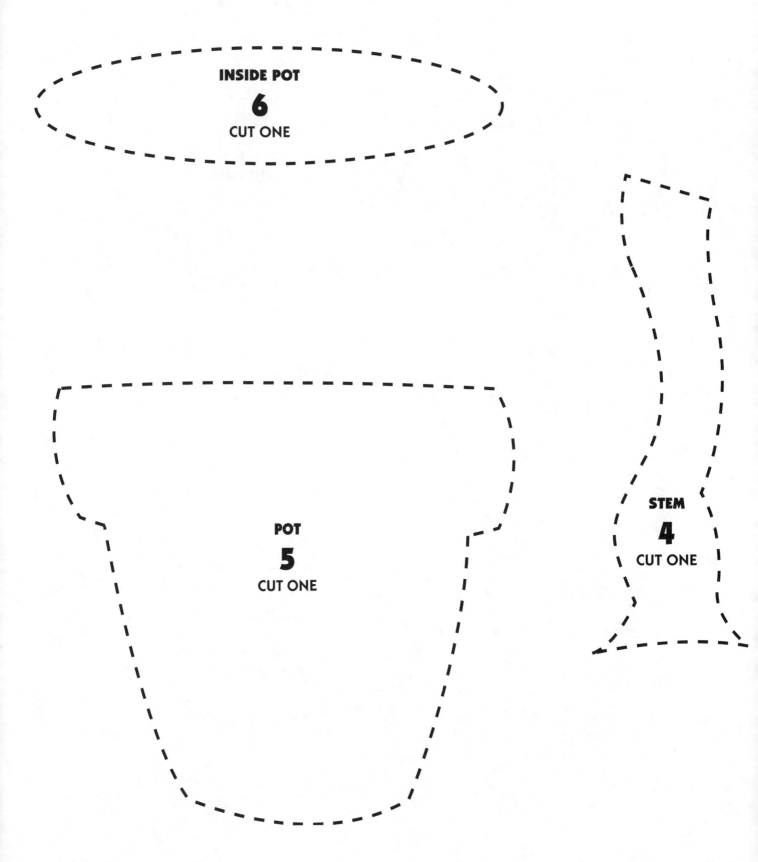

INSIDE POT

6

CUT ONE

POT

5

CUT ONE

STEM

4

CUT ONE

WATERING CAN

Materials: green, blue, white, red and brown paper; scissors; glue; black crayon or marker

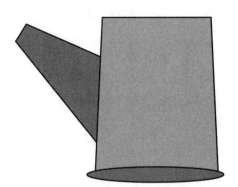

1 Cut one #1 can from green paper. Cut one #2 spout and one #3 base from blue paper. Glue the spout on the left side of the can. Glue the base at the bottom of the can.

2 Cut one #4 top handle and one #5 handle from white paper. Glue the top handle at the top of the can. Glue the handle on the right side of the can. Use a black crayon or marker to draw a line to complete the handle as shown.

3 Cut one #6 cap and one #7 stripe from blue paper. Glue the cap on the end of the spout. Glue the stripe on the middle of the can as shown. Use a black crayon or marker to draw small holes on the cap.

4 Cut one #8 ladybug from red paper and one #9 worm from brown paper. Glue the ladybug near the top of the watering can. Glue the worm on the base of the can as shown. Use a black crayon or marker to draw spots and a line on the ladybug. Draw a face on the worm.

Watering Can

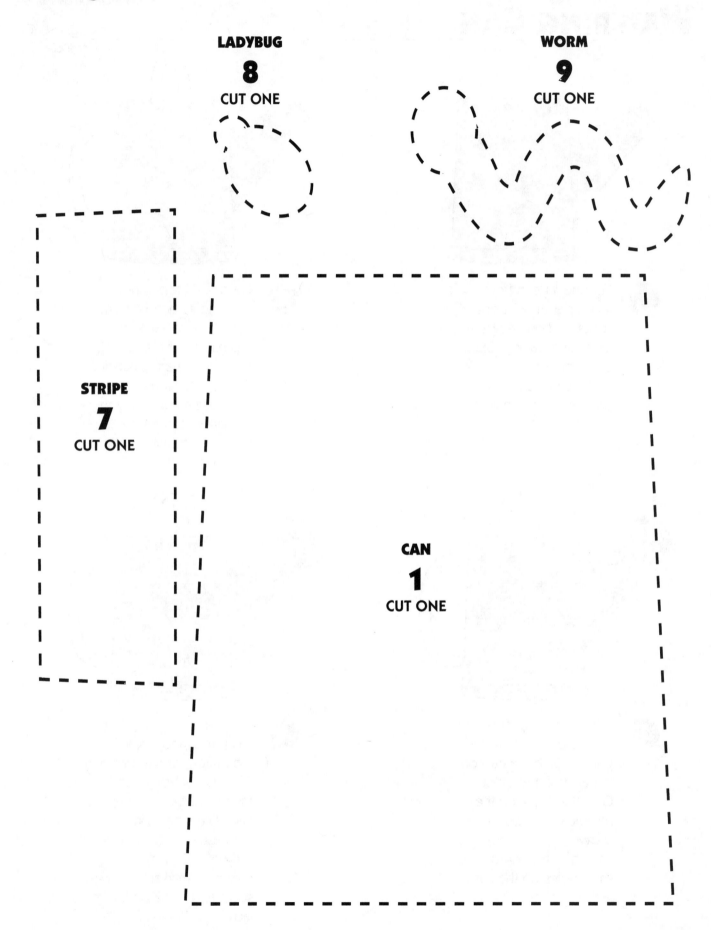

LADYBUG
8
CUT ONE

WORM
9
CUT ONE

STRIPE
7
CUT ONE

CAN
1
CUT ONE

Watering Can

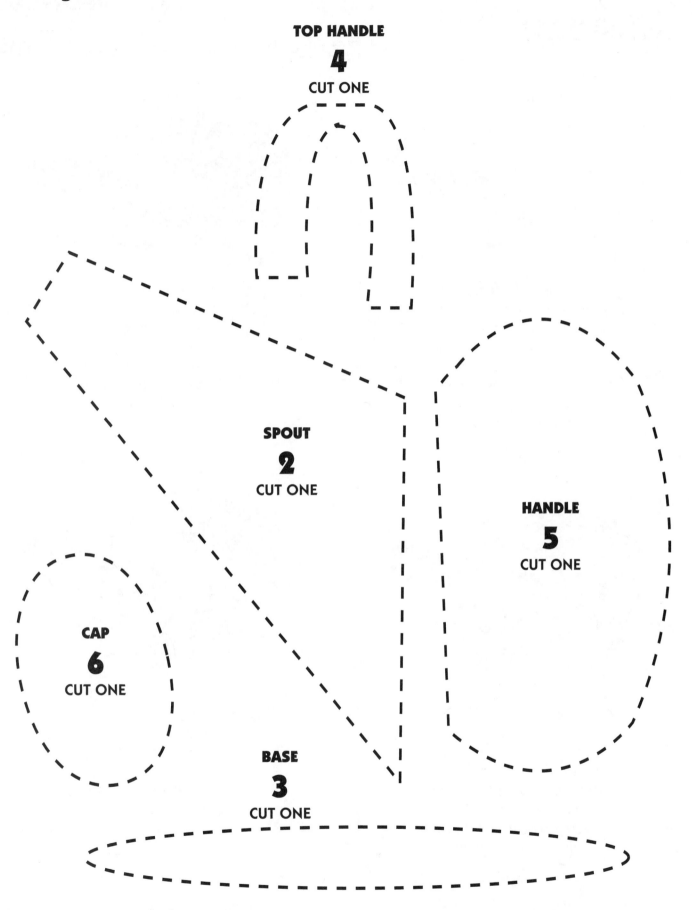

TOP HANDLE

4

CUT ONE

SPOUT

2

CUT ONE

HANDLE

5

CUT ONE

CAP

6

CUT ONE

BASE

3

CUT ONE

BASEBALL

Materials: *white, brown, red, light brown, black and white paper; scissors; glue; black crayon or marker; red crayon or marker*

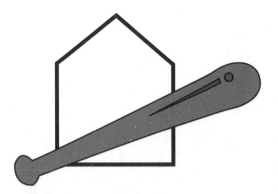

1 Cut one #1 home plate from white paper. Cut one #2 bat from brown paper. Use a black crayon or marker to draw markings on the bat as shown. Glue the bat on home plate as shown.

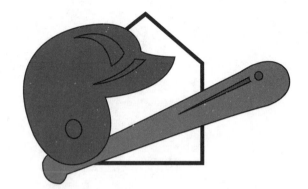

2 Cut one #3 helmet from red paper. Use a black crayon or marker to draw markings on the helmet as shown. Glue the helmet to the home plate and bat as shown.

3 Cut one #4 glove from light brown paper. Cut one #5 webbing from black paper. Glue the webbing between the thumb and first finger on the glove. Use a black crayon or marker to draw stitches between the fingers on the glove. Glue the glove on the bat as shown.

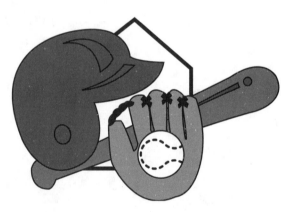

4 Cut one #6 baseball from white paper. Use a red crayon or marker to draw stitch marks on the ball as shown. Glue the baseball to the center of the glove.

Baseball

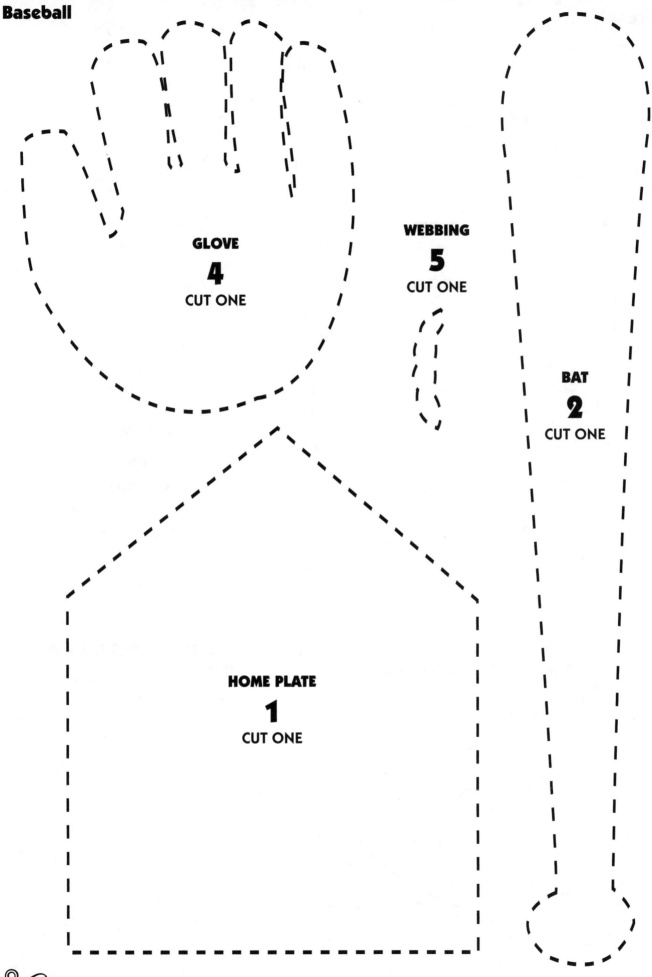

GLOVE
4
CUT ONE

WEBBING
5
CUT ONE

BAT
2
CUT ONE

HOME PLATE
1
CUT ONE

Baseball

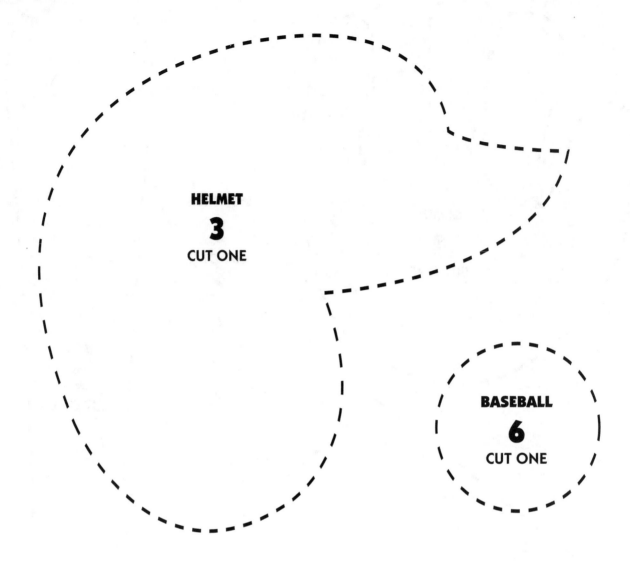

HELMET

3

CUT ONE

BASEBALL

6

CUT ONE

HELMET MARKINGS PATTERN

Note:
This is how the helmet markings are rendered.
Use this to trace or copy.

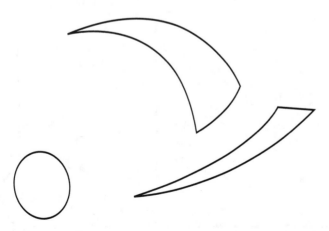

STITCH MARKS PATTERN

Note:
This is how the stitch marks are rendered.
Use this to trace or copy.

BIRD IN A NEST

Materials: light brown, light blue, orange, brown, white and black paper; scissors; glue; black crayon or marker

1 Cut one #1 nest and one #2 nest hole from light brown paper. Glue the nest hole on the nest as shown. Use a black crayon or marker to draw lines on the nest as shown.

2 Cut three #3 eggs from light blue paper. Glue the eggs on the nest hole. Cut one #4 body from orange paper. Glue the body to the left side of the nest.

3 Cut one each of #5 head, #6 tail and #7 wing from brown paper. Glue the head to the top of the body. Glue the tail at the end of the body. Glue the wing on the body as shown.

4 Cut one #8 beak from orange paper. Glue the beak on the head as shown. Cut one #9 eye from white paper and one #10 pupil from black paper. Glue the pupil on the eye. Then glue the eye on the head. Use a black crayon or marker to draw the line on the beak as shown.

Bird in a Nest

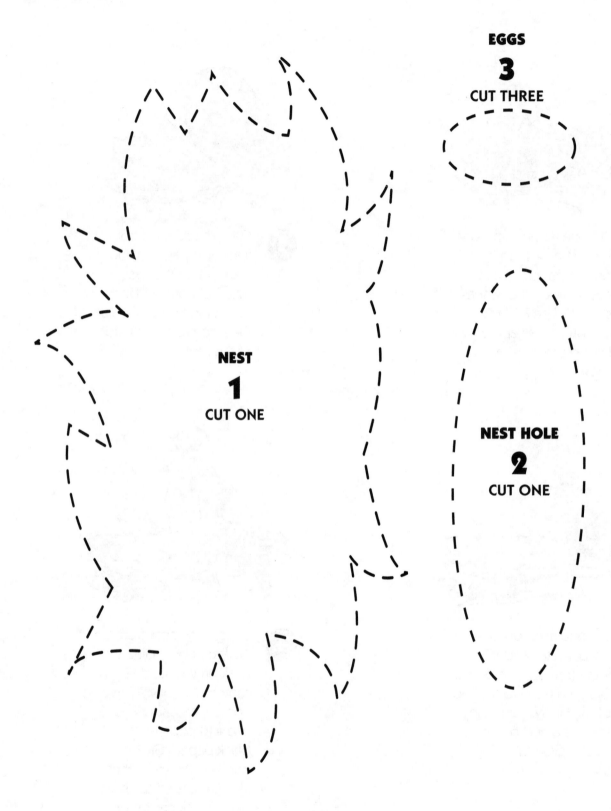

EGGS

3

CUT THREE

NEST

1

CUT ONE

NEST HOLE

2

CUT ONE

Bird in a Nest

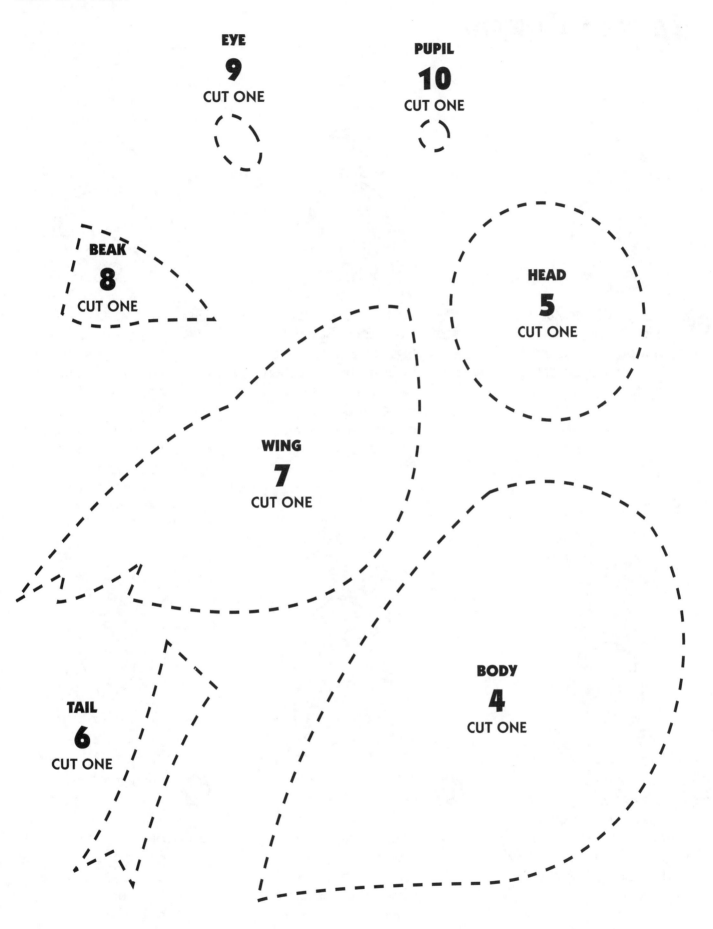

EYE
9
CUT ONE

PUPIL
10
CUT ONE

BEAK
8
CUT ONE

HEAD
5
CUT ONE

WING
7
CUT ONE

TAIL
6
CUT ONE

BODY
4
CUT ONE

EASTER BUNNY

Materials: *gray, white, yellow, blue, orange, light green, white and black paper; scissors; glue; black crayon or marker*

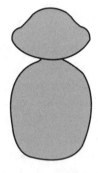

1 Cut one #1 body and one #2 head from gray paper. Glue the head on the top of the body.

2 Cut two #3 legs from gray paper. Glue the legs to the sides of the body as shown. Cut one #4 belly from white paper. Glue it on the center of the body.

3 Cut two #5 arms from gray paper. Glue the arms to the sides of the body near the top. Cut one each of #6 left ear and #7 right ear from gray paper. Glue the ears on top of the head as shown. Use a black crayon or marker to draw lines on the ears as shown.

4 Cut one #8 basket from yellow paper. Glue the basket on the bottom of the bunny. Use a black crayon or marker to draw lines on the basket as shown.

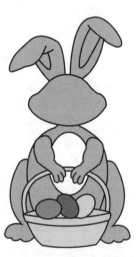

5 Cut three #9 eggs, one each from blue, orange and light green paper. Glue the eggs in the basket. Cut one #10 handle from yellow paper. Glue the handle to the basket and under the bunny's paws.

6 Cut two #11 eyes from white paper and two #12 pupils from black paper. Glue the pupils on the eyes. Then glue them on the bunny's face. Draw the nose and mouth with a black crayon or marker as shown.

60

Easter Bunny

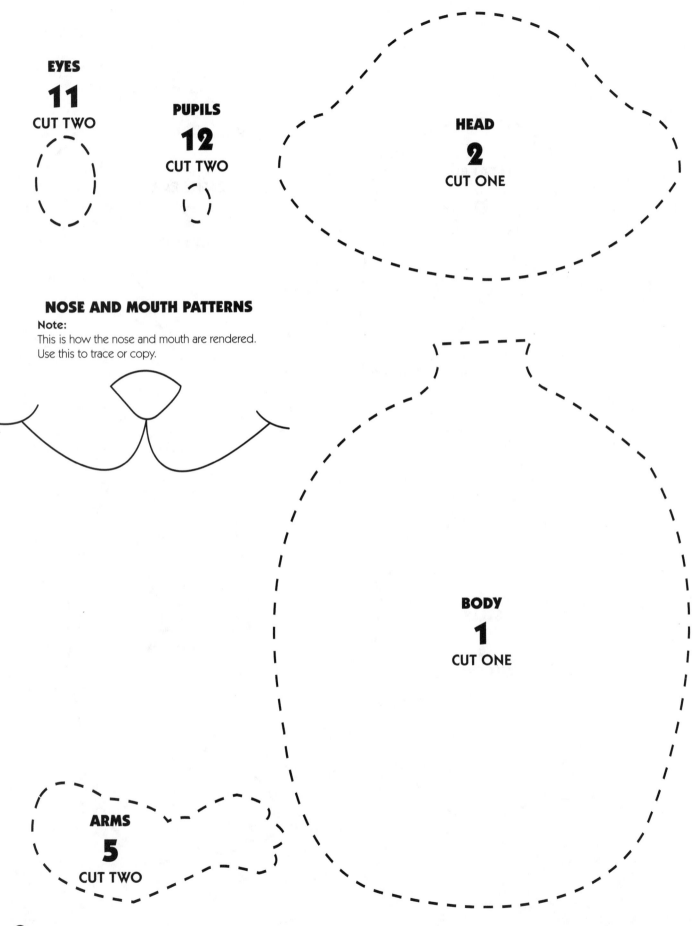

EYES

11

CUT TWO

PUPILS

12

CUT TWO

HEAD

2

CUT ONE

NOSE AND MOUTH PATTERNS

Note:
This is how the nose and mouth are rendered.
Use this to trace or copy.

BODY

1

CUT ONE

ARMS

5

CUT TWO

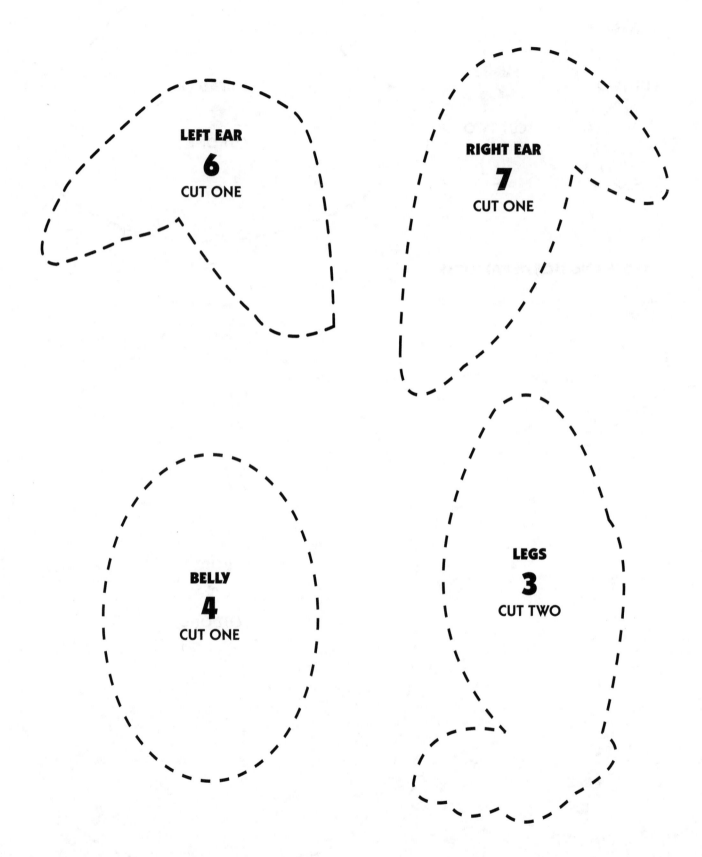

LEFT EAR
6
CUT ONE

RIGHT EAR
7
CUT ONE

BELLY
4
CUT ONE

LEGS
3
CUT TWO

HANDLE

10

CUT ONE

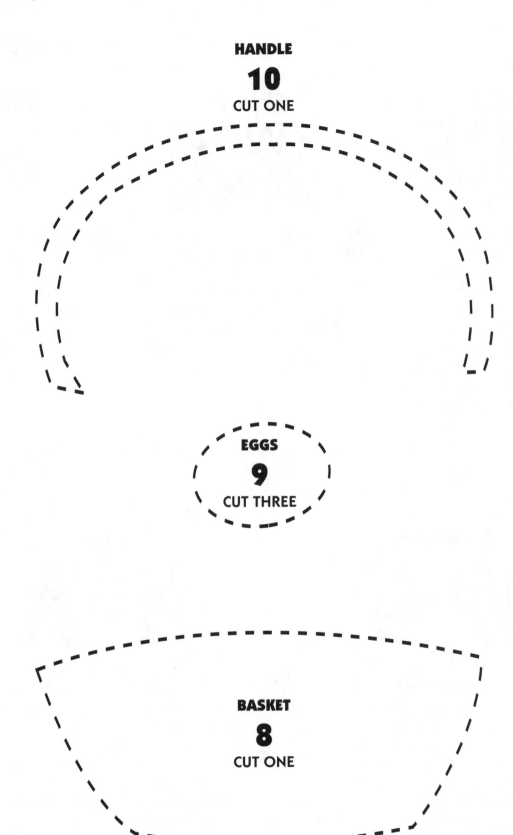

EGGS

9

CUT THREE

BASKET

8

CUT ONE

FLAGS

USA

1 Cut one #1 background from white paper. Cut seven #2 stripes from red paper. Glue the stripes on the background as shown. Cut one #3 field from blue paper. Place 50 gold star stickers on the blue corner. Glue the field on the upper left corner of the flag.

CHINA

2 Cut one #1 background from red paper. Cut one #4 China star and four #5 small stars from yellow paper. Glue the stars on the left side of the flag as shown.

JAPAN

2 Cut one #1 background from white paper. Cut one #6 Japan circle from red paper. Glue the red circle to the center of the white background.

CANADA

4 Cut one #1 background from white paper. Cut two #7 sides and one #8 maple leaf from red paper. Glue one of the sides on each end of the white background. Glue the maple leaf in the center of the flag.

MEXICO

5 Cut one #1 background from white paper. Cut two #7 sides, one from red paper and one from green paper. Glue the green side on the left end of the background and the red side on the right. Copy the #9 Mexico center onto white paper. Use crayons or markers to color it the following way:

eagle head, wing and tail—brown
eagle breast and feet—yellow
garlands—green with red berries and bow
snake in the eagle's beak—light green

Cut out the colored center and glue it to the center of the flag as shown.

BACKGROUND

1

CUT ONE

STRIPES

2

CUT SEVEN

MAPLE LEAF

8

CUT ONE

FIELD

3

CUT ONE

TLC10535 Copyright © Teaching & Learning Company, Carthage, IL 62321-0010

Flags

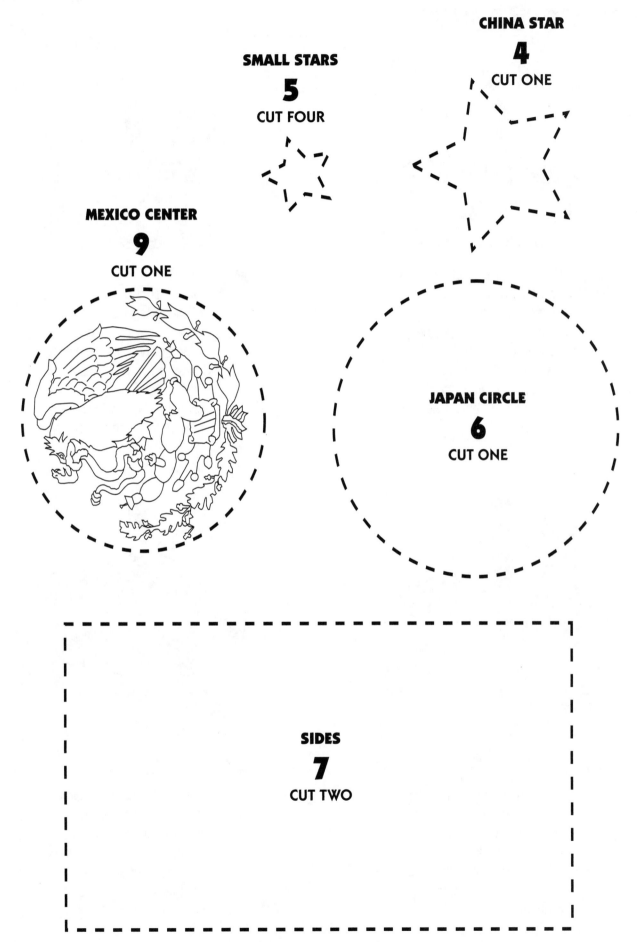

CHINA STAR

4

CUT ONE

SMALL STARS

5

CUT FOUR

MEXICO CENTER

9

CUT ONE

JAPAN CIRCLE

6

CUT ONE

SIDES

7

CUT TWO

PICNIC BASKET

Materials: yellow, dark brown, light brown, white, red and black paper; scissors; glue; black crayon or marker

1 Cut one #1 basket from yellow paper and one #2 handle from dark brown paper. Glue the handle on the top of the basket. Use a black crayon or marker to draw lines on the handle as shown.

2 Cut two #3 loaves of bread and one #4 chicken leg from light brown paper. Use a black crayon or marker to draw lines on the bread and chicken leg as shown. Glue the bread and chicken leg sticking out of the basket as shown.

3 Cut one #5 blanket from white paper. Cut seven #6 blanket squares from red paper. Glue the red squares on the blanket as shown to make it checkered. Glue the picnic basket on the blanket.

4 Cut two #7 ants from black paper. Glue one ant on the basket. Glue the other ant on the blanket. Use a black crayon or marker to draw lines for the antennas and feet on the ants as shown.

Picnic Basket

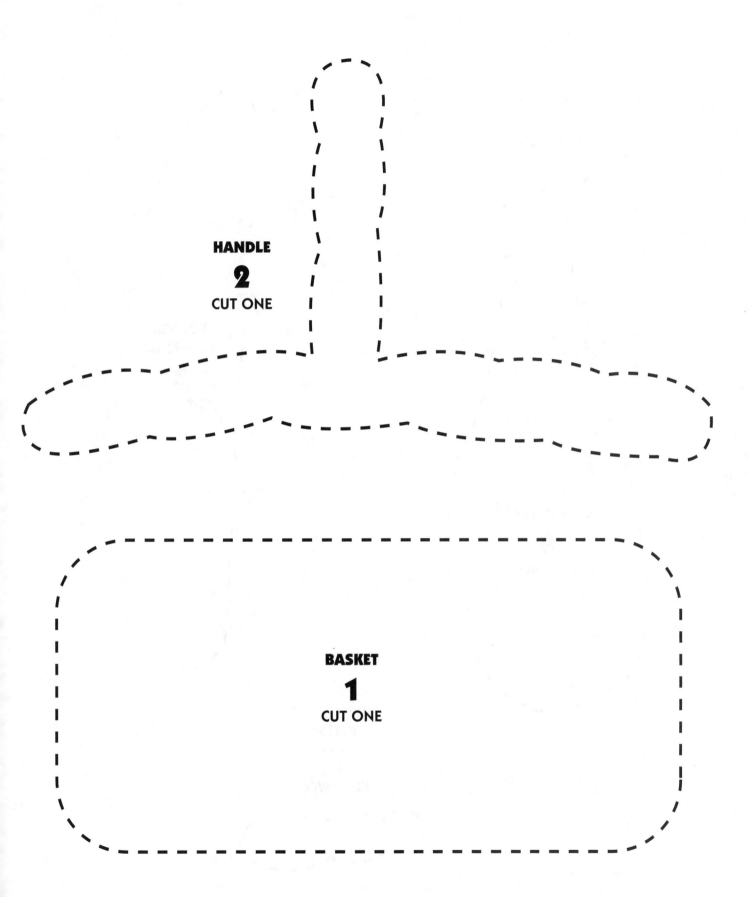

HANDLE

2

CUT ONE

BASKET

1

CUT ONE

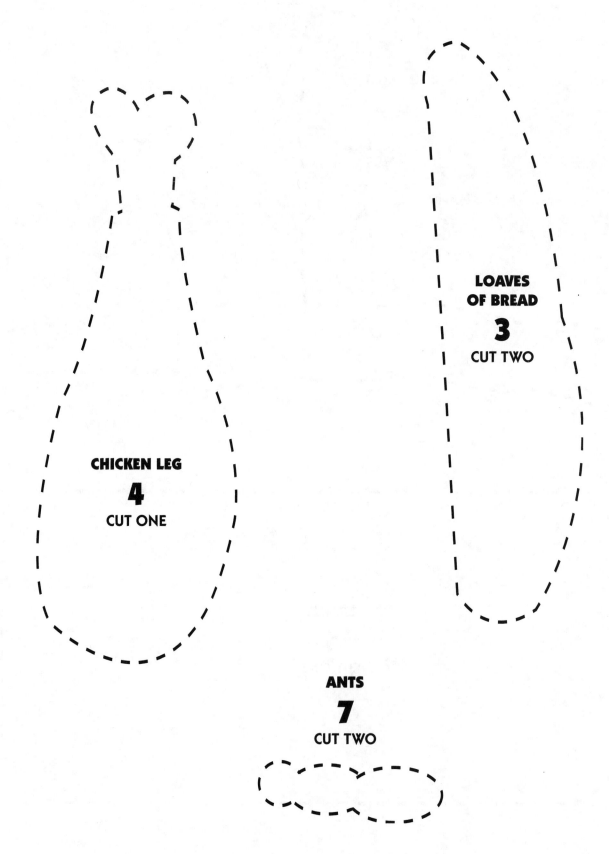

LOAVES
OF BREAD
3
CUT TWO

CHICKEN LEG
4
CUT ONE

ANTS
7
CUT TWO

Picnic Basket

BLANKET SQUARES
6
CUT SEVEN

BLANKET
5
CUT ONE

RAIN GEAR

Materials: *yellow, orange, tan or beige, black and blue paper; scissors; glue; black crayon or marker*

1 Cut one #1 coat from yellow paper. Cut one #2 collar from orange paper. Glue the collar on the top of the coat. Use a black crayon or marker to draw lines on the coat and cuffs on the sleeves as shown.

2 Cut one #3 head and one #4 neck from tan or beige paper. Cut one #5 hair from black paper. Glue the neck on the coat, then glue the head on the neck. Glue the hair on the head as shown.

3 Cut one #6 rain hat from yellow paper. Glue the hat on the girl's hair. Cut two #7 gloves from orange paper. Glue the gloves at the end of the sleeves. Cut several #8 buttons from orange paper. Glue the buttons on the raincoat. (You could use real buttons in place of the paper ones.) Use a black crayon or marker to draw lines on the hat and holes on the buttons as shown.

4 Cut two #9 boots from orange paper. Glue them at the bottom of the raincoat as shown. Cut several #10 raindrops from blue paper. Glue the raindrops on the rain hat. Use a black crayon or marker to draw on eyes, nose and mouth.

Rain Gear

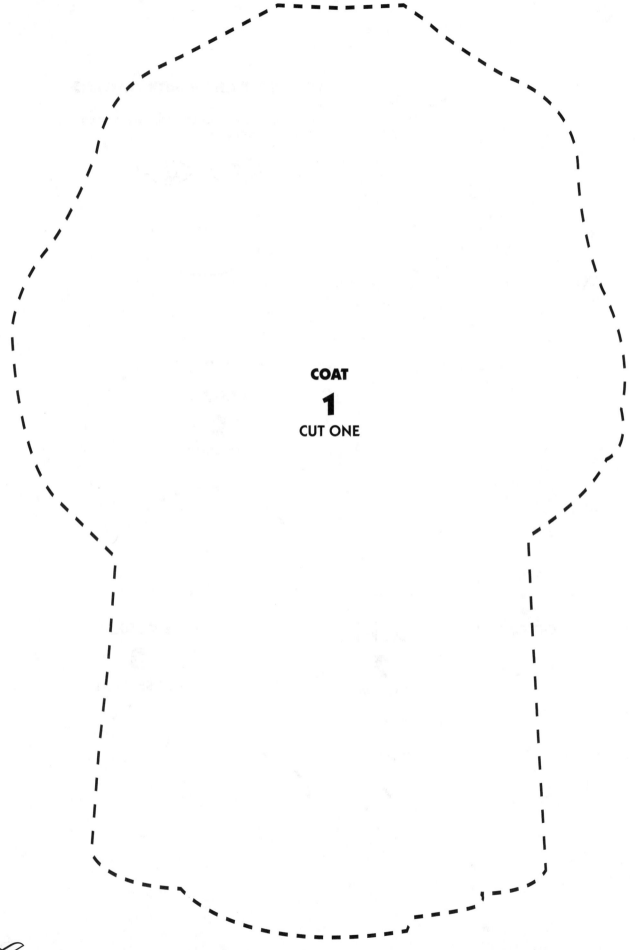

COAT
1
CUT ONE

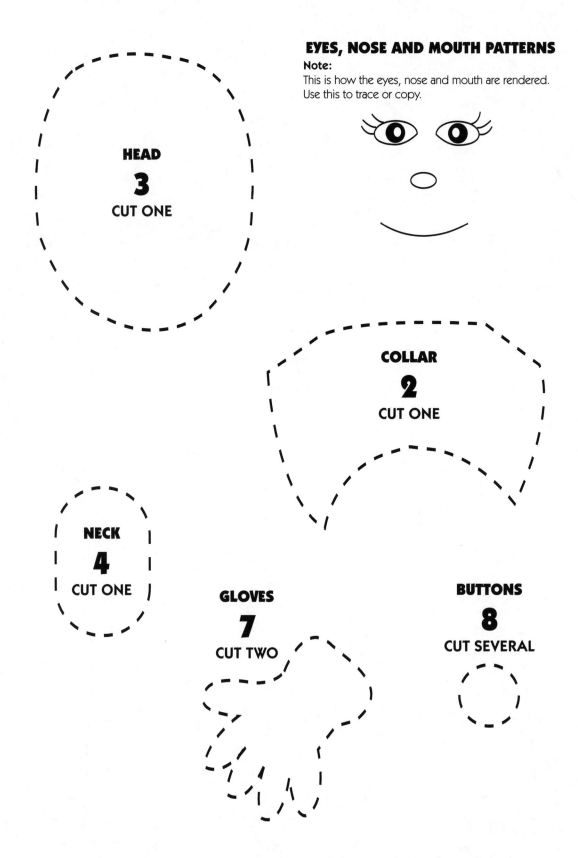

EYES, NOSE AND MOUTH PATTERNS

Note:
This is how the eyes, nose and mouth are rendered.
Use this to trace or copy.

HEAD
3
CUT ONE

COLLAR
2
CUT ONE

NECK
4
CUT ONE

GLOVES
7
CUT TWO

BUTTONS
8
CUT SEVERAL

Rain Gear

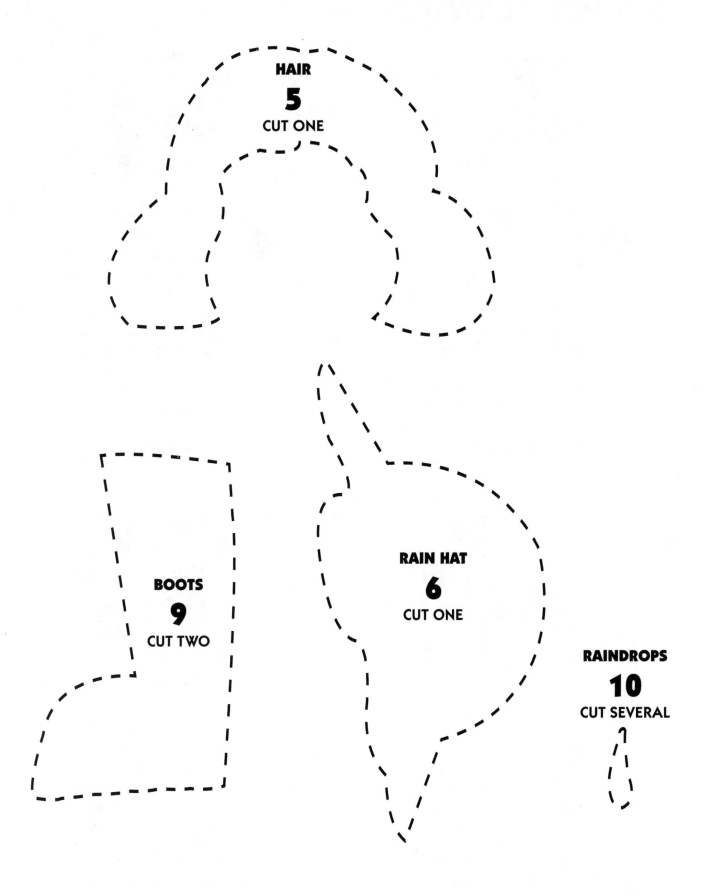

HAIR

5

CUT ONE

BOOTS

9

CUT TWO

RAIN HAT

6

CUT ONE

RAINDROPS

10

CUT SEVERAL

Summer Flowers

Materials: *blue, green, white, yellow, light green, purple and pink paper; scissors; glue; black crayon or marker*

1 Cut one #1 bowl from blue paper. Cut two #2 daisy leaves and one #3 daisy stem from green paper. Cut one #4 daisy petals from white paper. Glue the daisy petals on the stem and the stem to the top of the bowl. Glue one leaf on the stem and one on the edge of the bowl as shown. Use a black crayon or marker to draw lines on the daisy and the leaves as shown.

2 Cut two #5 daffodils from yellow paper. Cut two #6 daffodil stems and one #7 daffodil leaf from light green paper. Glue each daffodil to a stem. Glue the stems to the edges of the bowl. Glue the daffodil leaf on the daffodil stem as shown. Use a black crayon or marker to draw lines on the daffodils as shown.

3 Cut two #8 pansies from purple paper. Cut one #9 pansy stem from green paper. Glue one pansy to its stem and the stem to the bowl. Glue the other pansy to the edge of the bowl on top of the daisy leaf as shown. Use a black crayon or marker to draw lines on the pansies as shown.

4 Cut two #10 rosebuds from pink paper. Cut two #11 rose stems and one #12 rosebud leaf from light green paper. Use a black crayon or marker to draw lines on the rosebuds and leaf as shown. Glue the rosebuds to their stems. Glue a leaf on one stem. Then glue the rosebuds in the bowl as shown.

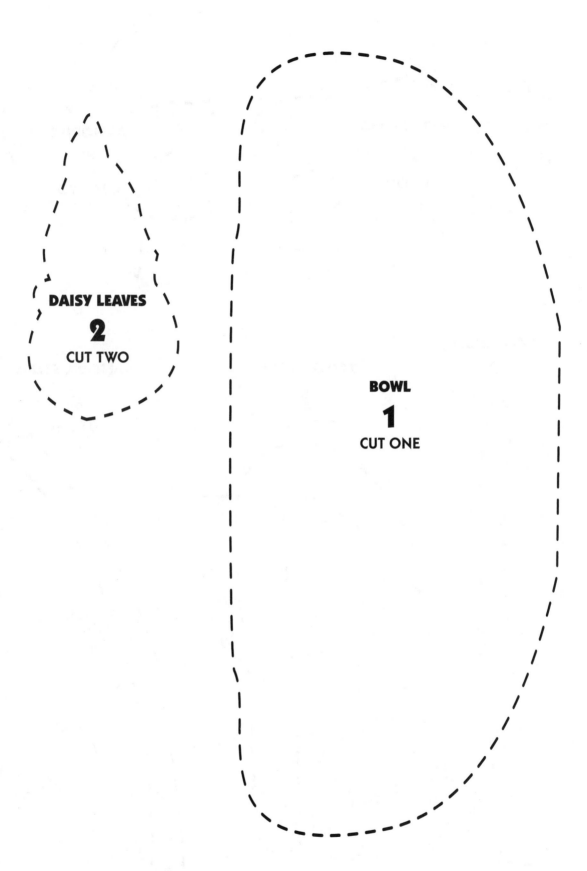

DAISY LEAVES

2

CUT TWO

BOWL

1

CUT ONE

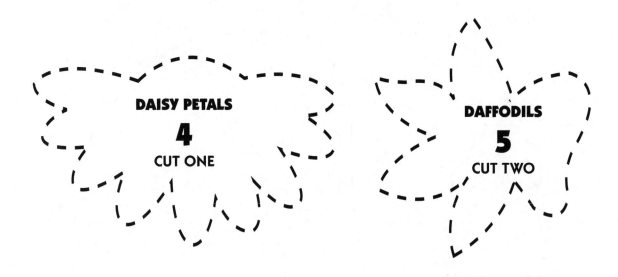

DAISY PETALS
4
CUT ONE

DAFFODILS
5
CUT TWO

DAISY STEM
3
CUT ONE

DAFFODIL LEAF
7
CUT ONE

DAFFODIL STEMS
6
CUT TWO

Summer Flowers

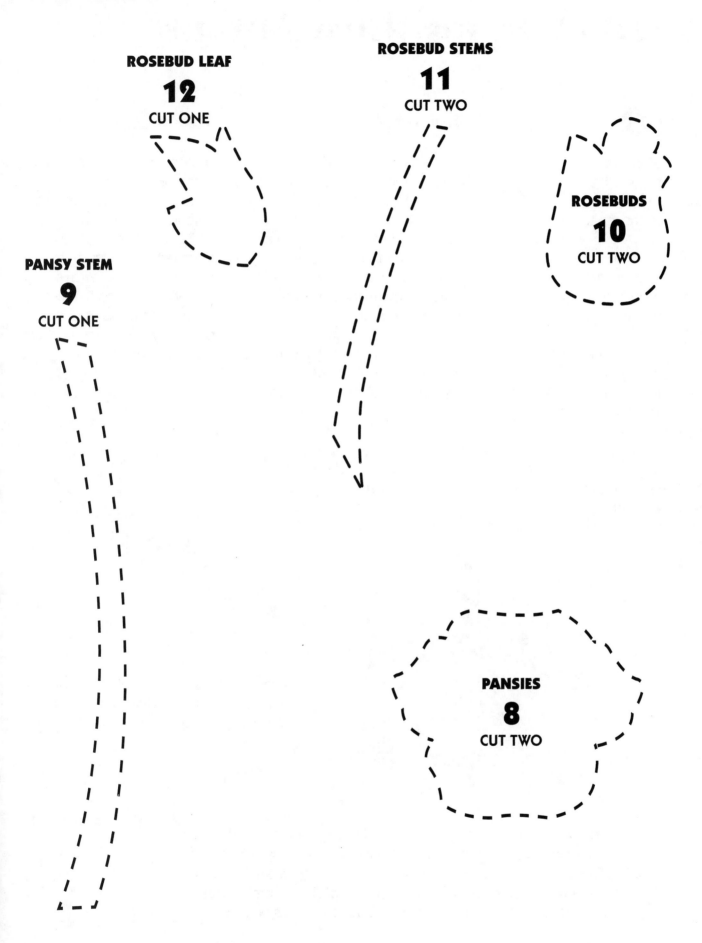

ROSEBUD LEAF
12
CUT ONE

ROSEBUD STEMS
11
CUT TWO

ROSEBUDS
10
CUT TWO

PANSY STEM
9
CUT ONE

PANSIES
8
CUT TWO

SUGGESTIONS FOR USING PATTERNS

Option 1

Cut one of each pattern piece. Trace the pieces on poster board, or any other sturdy paper thin enough to cut with scissors. Copy the information printed on each pattern piece to the poster board piece. Make as many sets as you need for your students. Let them trace around the poster board patterns to make the Cut and Create projects. Make a copy of the directions page for each project so students will have a step-by-step, visual guide to show them how to "build" it. Laminate the directions pages to make them more durable. You'll need one directions page for every set of patterns. Store each set in a zip-close plastic bag.

Option 2

To quickly prepare a Cut and Create project for one or two students, tape the pattern page(s) to a window or light box. Tape a sheet of paper over the patterns and trace them. Number the pattern pieces and indicate how many copies of each one the student needs to cut. Edit out any patterns you feel are too small for your students to manipulate. Make a copy of the directions page for each student. Give each student a copy of the traced patterns, the directions page and the materials list and they'll be ready to create!

Option 3

Photocopy the patterns directly onto colored paper. Cut out the pattern pieces and arrange them by color onto one sheet of white paper. Photocopy a set of these pattern pages on the colored paper for each student. You will also need to make several photocopies of the directions page, one for each group of students.

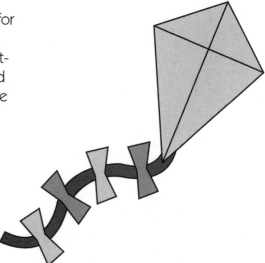

Note: Any eye or other small pieces that you feel are too difficult for students to handle may be drawn on with crayon or marker.

Note: Laminate your students' Cut and Create projects to keep them from getting bent or torn. You may want to staple or glue some of the projects to paint or craft sticks and put them in the drama corner, prop box or next to an appropriate story in the classroom library. Your students can use them to role-play and act out stories or poems.

Teaching & Learning Company
What Every Classroom Needs!
Poster Papers
Created for Kids to Complete!

Each two-sided, black and white poster folds open to 22" x 17".

30 per package

Front

Center

Back

Amazing ME
TLC10038 preK-2

Front

Center

My Very Own SCRAPBOOK

Back

It's Been a Great Year!
TLC10493 K-3

Manners, Please!
TLC10458 K-3

Building Character
TLC10492 K-3

Welcome Back to School
preK-K
TLC10285 preK-K

Welcome Back to School
Grades 1-3
TLC10285 Grades 1-3

Four Square Writing Method
TLC10415 Grades 4-6

Math Is Fun!
TLC10460 Grades 1-3

We Love America
TLC10320 K-3

My 5 Senses
TLC10509 K-3

Seasons
TLC10477 K-3

Weather
TLC10497 K-3

Telling Time
TLC10478 K-3

Money
TLC10508 Grades 1-3

Satisfaction Guaranteed

Teaching & Learning Company

Save on shipping and handling!
Contact your local school supply store for Teaching & Learning Company products. If there is no store in your community, write to:
Teaching & Learning Company, 1204 Buchanan St., P.O. Box 10, Carthage, IL 62321-0010. Thank you!

IBCP-07A

The simple yet creative projects in this book will help young children learn how to:
- follow directions
- hone fine-motor skills
- challenge and develop fine motor skills

The colorful finished products can be used for:
- stick puppets
- wall art
- bulletin boards
- class books
- literature companions
- vocabulary builders
- and dozens of other engaging, motivating activities.

So sharpen those scissor skills—it's time to Cut and Create!

Cut and Create! Spring & Summer

Author: Mary Tucker

Mary Tucker is a freelance writer, but considers herself a teacher who writes. She has enjoyed working with kids for many years as a teacher, a teacher's associate, a one-on-one tutor and a Sunday School teacher. She has written for kids of all ages. Mary lives in Iowa where she enjoys reading, music and walking her dog Digby.

Illustrator: Kim Rankin

Kim Rankin lives in a small midwest town with her husband, Robert. They are the proud parents of two daughters, Jessica Elizabeth and Megan Emily.

Kim has worked in educational publishing for over 15 years in typesetting, design and layout. She is a talented craftsperson and creates original, one-of-a-kind jewelry. She enjoys working on projects with her daughters and also finds time for a full-time free-lance career.

Cut and Create! Books

ISBN 978-1-57310-535-4

Teaching & Learning Company
1204 Buchanan St., P.O. Box 10, Carthage, IL 62321-0010

T3-BMR-418

Illinois Library Association

TRUSTEE FACTS FILE
Fourth Edition

Robert P. Doyle and
Robert N. Knight

Editors